Culinary MEXICO

Culinary MEXICO

Authentic Recipes and Traditions

DANIEL HOYER

Photography by Marty Snortum

Gibbs Smith, Publisher
Salt Lake City

First Edition
09 08 07 06 05   5 4 3 2 1

Text © 2005 Daniel Hoyer
Photographs © 2005 Marty Snortum

Published by
Gibbs Smith, Publisher
P.O. Box 667
Layton, Utah 84041

Orders: 1.800.748.5439
www.gibbs-smith.com

Designed by Dawn DeVries Sokol
Produced by Mary Ellen Thompsen
Printed and bound in Hong Kong

Library of Congress Cataloging-in-Publication Data
Hoyer, Daniel.
  Culinary Mexico : authentic recipes and traditions / Daniel Hoyer ; photographs by
Marty Snortum.-- 1st ed.
       p. cm.
  Includes index.
  ISBN 1-58685-375-9
  1. Cookery, Mexican. 2. Food habits--Mexico. I. Title.
TX716.M4H69 2005
641.5972--dc22
                              2005012296

Dedicated to

Ian Hoyer

November 9, 1985-July 30, 2004

Ian, you more than anyone else, always believed in me. If not for your constant encouragement and nonjudgmental support, I might never have completed this book. You were never afraid and I continue to draw strength from you. I miss you sorely and treasure your memory. I can still see your smile, taste your cooking, and hear your music every day. You deeply touched so many people, so much more than you ever realized. I will always wonder what more you might have accomplished. I love you with all my heart. Peace.

Contributions to the Ian Hoyer Memorial Music Fund may be sent to:
Chamisa Mesa Educational Center
P.O. Box 759
Ranchos de Taos, New Mexico 87557
(505) 751–0943

Contents

La Costa Oro, The Pacific Coast / 54

El Istmo, The Isthmus of Tehuantepec / 74

La Encrucijada, The Central Crossroads / 114

El Centro Colonial, The Colonial Plains and Highlands / 146

La Tierra Maya, The Yucatán Peninsula / 172

Acknowledgments

THE TASK OF THANKING EVERYONE WHO HAS HELPED ME OVER THE years to get to where I am now is daunting to say the least. So many people have contributed to my knowledge, and many others have provided inspiration, support, and encouragement, that it is difficult to know where to start. To those of you I fail to mention below, thank you; I am sorry to omit your names but please know that you are appreciated.

To Nancy: your love, support, and steadiness have always been there to keep me on track. Thanks for taking care of the details of life while I get lost in my projects and for being a willing test subject for my cooking.

Tristan, thank you for your interest in and your unquestioning acceptance of my life choices. I am sorry that I monopolized the computer so much. You continue to amaze me.

Thanks to my grandmothers and my mom for letting me follow them in the kitchen as a young boy, full of incessant questions; also, for trusting me to make the mashed potatoes and gravy for Sunday dinners.

To Beto and Doug, thanks for joining me on an important leg of my journey.

To all of the people I have worked with in restaurants over the years—co-workers, bosses, and employees, and especially my amigos y compadres Mexicanos: You have taught me most of what I know about food.

Many chefs and cookbook authors have inspired, guided, and informed me throughout my cooking career, most notably Rick Bayless, Diana Kennedy, Mark Miller, Patricia Quintana, Susana Trilling, Iliana de la Vega, Marilyn Tausend, Julia Child, and James Beard.

A special thank you to Susan, Nicole, Noe, and all of the staff and chefs at the Santa Fe School of Cooking. You have presented me with many opportunities, shared your secrets, and become an extended part of my family.

To Jennifer Grillone, this book's editor: You have maintained a positive and cheerful presence throughout my creative ups and downs and life's tragedies. Thanks for your patience.

I also wish to express my deep appreciation to all of the cooks in Mexico, from the distant past all the way to the present, who have contributed to the creation, development, and preservation of this magnificent cuisine.

Finally, thanks to Roy, David, Rafa, Doña Angela, Doña Rafaela, Doña Carmen, Erica, Maximiliano, and hundreds of other wonderful people who helped me in the discovery of my affinity to and love for the incredible land of Mexico.

Introduction

WHAT DO MOST NORTH AMERICANS AND EUROPEANS THINK OF when asked to describe Mexico? Mariachi music and picturesque beaches with palm trees waving in the wind; cactus, tequila, and margaritas; Pancho Villa, Hernán Cortez, Agustín Lara, and Montezuma; ancient pyramid ruins and colonial cathedrals; bullfights; and, of course, spicy food.

These images are all part of Mexico; however, when it comes to the food, there is much more to Mexico's gastronomy than tacos, enchiladas, burritos, and refried beans, all covered with melted cheese. Until recently, much of the Mexican food served north of the border and in Europe had been adapted to suit the tastes of "gringos" and was narrowly focused, given the limited availability of ingredients as well as the incomplete knowledge of restaurant owners regarding diverse preparation techniques.

The stereotypical view of Mexican cuisine is beginning to change as more and more emigrants from Mexico are settling in communities throughout the United States. Moreover, Mexico has become a very popular travel destination for Americans as well as Europeans. Many chefs have been discovering the wide range of flavors in authentic Mexican foods (helped, in part, by the fact that many Mexican emigrants have found employment as kitchen workers in U.S. restaurants).

Mexico has a rich history, a varied geography and climate, and a myriad of cultural influences that are reflected in its food. Contrast the barbacoa of the Central Colonial region with the black mole of Oaxaca and bring in the pork in orange sauce from the Yucatan and you might think that the dishes represent three completely different countries! In a way, they do. Each of these preparations were developed in their respective regions by the influences of available ingredients, trade practices, and local economies, and the cultures of indigenous peoples, explorers, colonial settlers, immigrants, and other countries that were trade partners.

In this book, I hope to help illuminate the rich diversity of Mexican cuisine by dividing the country (albeit arbitrarily) into six gastronomic regions.

- *La Frontera*, the states bordering the United States, Baja California, Sonora, Chihuahua, Coahuila, Nuevo León, and Tamaulipas
- *La Costa Oro*, the Pacific coast from Sinaloa to Guerrero
- *El Istmo*, the Isthmus of Tehuantepec, including the states of Tabasco, Oaxaca, and Veracruz
- *La Encrucijada*, the crossroads, comprising Mexico City and its surrounding states
- *El Centro Colonial*, the central plains and highlands with the stately colonial cities of Guadalajara, Zacatecas, San Miguel de Allende, Guanajuato, Querétaro, Morelia, and San Luis Potosí
- *La Tierra Maya*, including Chiapas, parts of Tabasco, and the Yucatán peninsula

Valid arguments could be made for a different division, and most of the listed areas could be divided further into six or more parts themselves. However, this regional profile suits my description of the various styles and reflects my personal experiences while traveling and studying in Mexico.

The history, traditions, and regional/cultural variations of Mexico's food and cooking make this a truly fascinating subject. The uniqueness of authentic Mexican food also derives from the innumerable individual styles and techniques that are used in its creation. I hope you will come to share my enthusiasm as you experience the recipes, ingredients, and tastes of this cookbook.

My appreciation for good Mexican food started when I was a child in my hometown of Topeka, Kansas. Although not well-known as a hotbed of Mexican gastronomy, it was a major hub of the Atchison, Topeka, and Santa Fe Railroad, and as such, had a long-thriving Mexican community that was first established when immigrant laborers were brought to help construct the railroad. I have fond memories of the Fiesta of Guadalupe each autumn and of the two restaurants,

La Siesta and Lucky Five. I will never forget the day in ninth grade when my football teammate Luis Tetuan brought a cooler full of tacos guisados to practice. Made by his mother, the tacos were soft-shelled and filled with chunks of braised meat, potatoes, carrots, and peas. What a revelation! Taco shells didn't need to be fried, you could fill them with things other than ground beef, and cheese was not a necessary addition!

My fascination with Mexican food continued to grow as I built my career in restaurants. Living in such states as Colorado, California, and Texas increased my exposure to different Mexican cooking styles. Moving to New Mexico, where I now live, put me face-to-face with the distinctiveness of New Mexican cooking. All this helped prepare me for the defining moment that opened me up to all the possibilities of the flavors and styles of true, authentic, regional Mexican cuisine: I was promoted to sous chef for Mark Miller's Coyote Café in Santa Fe. The Coyote Café was and is well-known for its modern southwestern cooking; however, southwestern cuisine is firmly rooted in the flavors, traditions, and techniques of Mexican cookery. Under Miller's fastidious tutelage, I developed a taste, an understanding, and an even greater appreciation for the nuances of Mexican flavors. Mark Miller was an anthropologist before he became a celebrity chef. As a result of his influence, I began to explore not only the cooking of Mexico, but the history and culture of this complex and intriguing country as well.

Enough of my story. Please join me on a journey of discovery through the varied geography, culture, history, and gastronomy of culinary Mexico.

Techniques and

Ingredients

GOOD MEXICAN COOKING STARTS WITH THE RIGHT INGREDIENTS prepared using the proper techniques. This chapter gives you advice and cooking techniques you will find useful for making the recipes in this book.

Substituting Ingredients

IN A PERFECT WORLD, all the ingredients for a given recipe would be readily available, in wonderful peak condition and of uniform flavor. In reality, the item called for may be out of season, not at its peak of ripeness, or just not convenient to obtain. Also, fresh food varies from plant to plant and region to region. Two chiles from the same plant may range from mild to fairly hot; normally tame poblano chiles sometimes may be fairly hot due to the season or where they were grown, and diverse varieties of tomatoes have different flavors—some are sweet, some are more acidic. Dried herbs and spices may also lose some intensity of flavor over time, depending on how they have been stored.

To cope with these challenges, cooks need to be flexible and use their taste buds along with their experience and a little intuition. A recipe provides a guideline that often needs interpretation and some adjustment. Good cooks also like to express their own personal style by varying recipes and substituting ingredients to suit their personal tastes and to please their guests.

In Mexico, many traditional recipes use terms like *bastante* (enough or sufficient), *enfriar* or *cocinar muy bien* (fry or cook well), and *al gusto* (as you like). The amounts given are often very ambiguous and allow for the cook's own interpretation. I encourage you to take liberties with the recipes in this book. In some recipes I have listed logical replacements for ingredients based on my tastes, but you should also feel free to make substitutions as you like. You may prefer spicier or milder, ancho chiles to guajillo chiles, more or less onions and garlic, sea bass instead of snapper, and so on. Please feel free to make the recipes your own. There is no right or wrong to great cooking if the results please the cook and his or her guests. In New Mexico we say *panza llena, corazón contento* (full belly, contented heart). If you can achieve that, you have successfully captured the Mexican way of cooking!

Sautéing

SAUTÉING EXPOSES INGREDIENTS to high temperatures to produce flavor, texture, and color. Many home cooks, and even restaurant cooks, often do not use a high enough setting in sautéing ingredients. Do not be afraid of the high setting on your stove when sautéing or frying. If you want to reduce the mess from splattering, you can use a high-sided pan or a splatter screen.

My rule of thumb for sautéing is "hot pan, cool oil." Preheat the pan before adding the oil, which is at room temperature. If you follow this rule, the food will not stick to the pan as much. Keep the temperature high and only reduce the heat if things start to burn. Do not overload the pan. Many meats and vegetables contain a lot of liquid, which cools the oil. An overly full pan will not maintain enough heat to achieve the desired results. Also, stirring cools down what you are cooking, so keep stirring to a minimum, especially when you first add ingredients to the hot oil.

Cooking Dry Beans

DRY BEANS ARE EASY TO COOK if you follow a few simple rules. First, sort the beans to remove any rocks, debris, or broken beans. Then rinse the beans well in cool water. Beans should be cooked completely before adding any salt or acidic ingredients such as vinegar, tomatoes, or pickled chiles. If these ingredients are added too soon, it can toughen the beans and make them difficult to cook through in a reasonable amount of time. After the beans are cooked to the point of tenderness with a consistent color throughout, you may season them and continue cooking to incorporate the flavors.

Cooking times will vary greatly depending on the variety and freshness of the beans, as well as the altitude, type of cooking pot used, and the temperature of your stove. I often use a pressure cooker for beans, which is especially useful at high altitudes. Most beans will cook completely in about 35 minutes at 15 pounds of pressure. In a regular pot, the times can range from 45 to 75 minutes at sea level to several hours at higher altitudes.

Presoaking beans will speed up the cooking process. Changing the water after soaking will help eliminate a little of the gassiness that beans may cause; however, it may also cause the beans to shed some of their skins and to break up more in the cooking process. I generally do not presoak beans before cooking unless I have a batch that is particularly dry. The use of fresh epazote to season beans is also reputed to help with the gassiness problem, but I find that thorough cooking is the most important factor.

Rinsing Onions

RAW ONIONS CAN DEVELOP a "gassy and hot" odor and flavor when used uncooked in salads and salsas, especially after time. To help prevent this, classic cookery uses the methods of either soaking onions in ice water for 30 to 45 minutes or blanching in boiling water and then quickly cooling. I recommend rinsing the onions since it is much quicker and easier, and the flavor and texture of a raw onion remains intact.

To use this method, simply place the cut onions in a strainer or sieve and rinse under hot tap water for 20 to 30 seconds while shaking them several times to ensure all the surfaces are exposed. Switch to cold water and rinse for the same amount of time or until the onions are cooled completely. Proceed with the recipe.

Roasting and Toasting

FIRE IS AN INDISPENSABLE ELEMENT in Mexican cookery. It is used with a comal or skillet to unlock the flavors of dried chiles, herbs, and other spices. Fire enriches the taste of tomatoes, tomatillos, garlic, and onions through caramelizing and charring. Fresh chiles, tomatillos, and tomatoes are frequently roasted over an open flame, which imparts an even more intense smokiness. (In this book I refer to *toasting* of dry ingredients such as seeds, herbs, and diced chiles. For fresh fruits and vegetables, I refer to the application of a direct flame as *roasting*.) The extra flavor and complexity achieved by roasting and toasting can be useful in many styles of cooking, not only Mexican. This application of intense heat also reduces the overall cooking times for many recipes, as a long simmering time is often unnecessary for full flavor development. If you learn only one new technique from this book, this is the most important. Roasting can improve the flavors in all of your cooking.

Fire-Roasting Fresh Chiles

FRESH CHILES ARE FIRE-ROASTED to remove the skin, to begin the cooking process before they are added to a dish, and to give them a smoky and slightly sweeter flavor. The larger varieties of chiles such as poblano, New Mexican green, and Anaheim are usually roasted and peeled. The smaller types like jalapeño, serrano, and habanero may be used raw, or they may be roasted and charred and then peeled and seeded for some sauces and salsas. (Sometimes the chiles are left intact after roasting.) This method also works for sweet bell peppers.

To fire-roast, place the chile over a direct flame or as near to a direct source of intense heat as possible (an open gas burner, charcoal or gas grill, oven broiler, or toaster oven) and char the skin until at least 80 to 90 percent of the skin is blistered and blackened. Rotate often to cook evenly.

Place the chile in a paper or plastic bag or in a bowl covered with a kitchen towel or plastic wrap to trap the steam. This will loosen the skin and continue

cooking the chile. After 10 to 15 minutes, rub the chile with a cloth or paper towel to remove the skin. I do not recommend rinsing in running water to remove the skin. Although that method is very efficient, the water also removes much of the flavor that you have been working so hard to create. After peeling, carefully slit open the chile on one side to remove the seeds. Remove seeds before stuffing for chile rellenos; remove stem and seeds before chopping to use in salsa or pureeing for a sauce or soup.

You may want to wear rubber gloves when handling the chiles to avoid burning your skin. Always remember to wash your hands well after peeling chiles. A vinegar rinse followed by soap and warm water works well. Do not touch your eyes or your skin before washing your hands or you may regret it!

Roasting Garlic

GARLIC CLOVES ARE ROASTED WHOLE to remove the raw taste and to sweeten the flavor. Roasted garlic is more subtle in flavor than fresh garlic, so you usually will need to use more than you would if you were using raw. Peeled garlic will roast more quickly and turn a darker color; unpeeled cloves tend to get sweeter when roasted and stay lighter in color. The choice is yours. I choose the method depending on the flavor I want.

Garlic is roasted like onions and the two may be roasted together. They require the same temperature; however, the timing may differ. Garlic is roasted at a higher temperature for a shorter time in Mexican cooking than it is in Italian cooking, so it does not get as soft.

Roasting Onions

IN MEXICAN COOKING, many recipes for salsas, sauces, and broths call for roasted onions. Roasting sweetens the onions, removing or reducing the "hot" taste of raw onions. Slightly charring the onions also produces a flavor that is complementary to roasted chiles, tomatoes, and tomatillos.

To roast onions, use a preheated comal, heavy skillet, or a cookie sheet in a 350-degree F oven. Roast 1/2-inch-thick slices or quarters of onions, turning occasionally until onions reach a golden-brown color (a little black around the edges is okay).

Toasting Dry Spices, Chiles, and Herbs

To TOAST DRY SPICES, CHILES, OR HERBS, preheat a comal, heavy skillet, or Dutch oven over a medium-high heat until you can feel the heat radiate from the surface (the surface should be 350 to 375 degrees F). Roast the coarser items such as whole chiles and seeds first, followed by herbs and leaves. Finish with ground spices and lastly, ground chiles. Finely ground spices have more surface area exposed to the heat so they are more likely to burn. Finish roasting quickly, as the chile smoke is irritating and may cause you to cough and sneeze. Ventilate your work area well!

Stir or toss frequently to allow even toasting. You want to lightly char, not scorch, the ingredients. When some smoke appears and color begins to develop, remove to a cool container or surface. Make sure to wipe out the pan before adding a new ingredient. You do not want to burn the remaining particles from the previous toasting. Only toast what you can use in your day's cooking; toasting releases the flavors in spices, herbs, and chiles, and by the next day there will not be much left.

Delicate "sweet" spices like cinnamon and cloves have such a volatile flavor that toasting can cause a loss of flavor, so I usually do not toast them. I toast allspice when used in savory dishes and not when used in sweet dishes.

Whole seeds may be ground in a mortar and pestle, spice grinder, or molcajete immediately after toasting. Herbs are usually added to recipes whole but sometimes are ground. Whole dry chiles are typically stemmed and seeded after they are toasted, and then soaked in enough very hot water (180 to 200 degrees F) to cover for 15 to 20 minutes to rehydrate them. The chiles are then drained before using in recipes.

Roasting Tomatoes and Tomatillos

BOTH TOMATOES AND TOMATILLOS MAY BE ROASTED or charred to improve their flavor for salsa, sauces, and soups. They may be flame-roasted to impart a smoky, slightly bitter, and charred quality, or they may be slowly pan-roasted on a comal, a well-seasoned skillet, or a baking sheet in a 350-degree F oven for a sweeter, more concentrated flavor. Pan-roasting may also be used to blacken the fruits, if you desire. This method also produces a more pronounced ripe flavor, which is useful for those almost flavorless, pink winter tomatoes.

Tomatillos need to be husked before roasting. Some cooks soak them to loosen the skin and remove the sticky substance from beneath the skin. I prefer to husk them dry and then rinse in very warm water for a few seconds to remove the stickiness.

For flame-roasting tomatillos and tomatoes, proceed as with fresh chiles until the desired degree of blackness is achieved. If you are using a pan or comal, preheat it to about 325 degrees F and place the tomatoes or tomatillos in the dry pan over a medium-low to medium flame. (The pan or comal should be well seasoned, but do not add oil. You are roasting, not frying.) Turn the tomatoes or tomatillos occasionally but not too often. Remove from heat when browned or blackened as desired and chop or puree as needed.

Making Tamale Wrappers

MOST TAMALES ARE WRAPPED either in dried cornhusks or banana leaves. If you cannot find one, you can always substitute the other. Dried cornhusks need to be soaked before using to make them pliable. To soak, place the husks in a bowl or pan deep enough to submerge them and add enough water to completely cover. (Hot water speeds up this process.) Soak for at least an hour and up to overnight. When you are ready to use the husks, drain them and then wipe off the excess water.

Banana leaves may be found, usually frozen, in Mexican and Latin groceries or Asian markets. To use, thaw first, then rinse well and wipe dry. Cut into pieces appropriate for the recipe that you are following. The leaves need to be lightly toasted before filling to make them pliable and to prevent splitting. Toast them over a direct flame or on a comal for a few seconds. You will notice the color of the banana leaf will change slightly as heat is applied, and the surface of the leaf will develop a shiny quality as it is toasted. Do not overtoast, as this will cause the leaf to become brittle. Cover the toasted leaves with a damp towel until you are ready to use them.

Making Tamale Masa

MANY RECIPES CALL FOR PREPARED MASA for tamales or nixtamal. This can be purchased at a tortillería or can be easily made at home using masa harina. To prepare masa for tamales, simply mix the quantity of dry masa harina called for with 1/2 to 2/3 of the same amount of very warm water or broth (120 to 150 degrees). Mix well and let sit, covered, for 20 to 30 minutes. Proceed with the recipe.

La Frontera

BAJA CALIFORNIA, SONORA, CHIHUAHUA, COAHUILA, NUEVO LEÓN, DURANGO, AND TAMAULIPAS

I HAVE PAINTED THIS REGION WITH A BROAD STROKE to include all of the states that border the United States. Excluding a few major cities, the population is sparsely distributed. Because of this, as well as the large areas of desert and grazing lands with extreme high and low temperatures, the cuisine that developed here is fairly simple and practical to better cope with the challenging living conditions.

Hunting once played an important role in this region, and many dishes here were created by men, in contrast to the rest of Mexico, where women exerted the greatest influence on cooking styles. Wheat is also important in the local diet, and most Norteños prefer flour tortillas over corn. You can find localized versions of typical Mexican fare in La Frontera, as well as many regional specialties that were influenced by the indigenous peoples and the traditions of the ranching culture that has existed here for centuries. Norteños use many different methods for food preservation: drying, pickling, conserving, fermentation, and candy making.

North-of-the-border visitors have also recently begun to influence the distinct Norteño style of cooking. Transient workers of southern Mexico heading to jobs in the United States, and immigrants with jobs in the tourist and manufacturing industries have also contributed to the local fare. German-speaking Mennonite people, who settled here in the past century, have added their cheese- and sausage-making techniques into the mix. People throughout Mexico enjoy Mennonite cheeses, and the Norteño chorizo bears the unmistakable stamp of German style.

La Frontera has bridged the ages of regional Mexican food. The simple, hearty ranch foods of the cattle country; the basic preparations of the indigenous hunter-gatherer Tarahumara of the spectacularly rugged Copper Canyon area; and the historical contributions of many ancient civilizations are the mainstays of this region. The modern, internationally influenced Mexican cuisine offered in the resorts of Baja, California, and cosmopolitan Monterey have added a distinctive flair to this region.

Queso Fundido

WARM CHEESE DIP

LITERALLY MEANING "MELTED CHEESE," Queso Fundido is a widely available appetizer at many restaurants in Mexico as well as in the United States. Many variations use different cheese selections, assorted flavorings, and additions. This version is my own, based on the many I have tasted around Mexico. When you get the hang of this recipe, you can experiment to make your own creations. Queso Fundido goes well with Guacamole (see page 69) and your favorite salsa.

MAKES 6 TO 8 SERVINGS AS AN APPETIZER

1. Lightly sauté the longaniza or chorizo in a little oil until cooked through and fat is fully rendered. (If using longaniza or chorizo in a casing, first remove the skin, and then cut into 1/2-inch pieces.) Drain in a strainer and reserve the fat.

2. Sauté the mushrooms on medium-high in the chorizo fat until nicely browned (if the chorizo is lean, you may need a little extra oil for the mushrooms). Add the chorizo, salt, epazote or oregano, and chiles and heat through, mixing well.

3. In a lightly oiled, oven-proof gratin dish, casserole, cast-iron skillet, or other pan (small for individual servings or large for family style), spread half of the cheese, then add an even layer of the mushroom mixture. Top with the remaining cheese, then the onion slivers.

4. Place under a broiler on high or in a 475-degree F oven until the cheese is bubbly and beginning to brown a little.

5. Serve immediately with warm flour tortillas cut in wedges.

1/2 pound longaniza or chorizo

1/2 pound mushrooms (white button, crimini, shiitake), sliced

Oil for sautéeing

Generous dash of salt

4 leaves fresh epazote, roughly chopped (or 1 to 2 tablespoons Mexican oregano, toasted)

1 or 2 thinly sliced chipotle chiles en adobo (or 1 ancho or guajillo chile, stemmed, seeded, toasted, and cut into thin strips, see page 25)

1 pound cheese (Mennonite, asadero, quesadilla, fontina, or Monterey Jack), shredded

1/2 white onion, cut into long slivers

Machaca Norteña
NORTHERN-STYLE SHREDDED BEEF

THIS BEEF PREPARATION is the basis of many dishes in Chihuahua and the rest of Mexico, including burritos, empanadas, soups, Machaca con Huevo, Ropa Vieja, Salpicon de Res, and so on. I have learned many variations from my amigos Chihuahuenses who live and work in restaurants around New Mexico. Often the beef is first boiled before shredding; however,
I prefer roasting it to concentrate the flavors and deepen the color.

MAKES 6 TO 8 MAIN COURSE SERVINGS OR 12 APPETIZERS

1. Season the roast with salt and pepper as well as oregano and chile powder (if using):

2. In a preheated heavy skillet, pour in a little oil, and then sear the meat well on all sides.

3. Place the meat in a roasting pan and distribute the vegetables and herbs under and on top of the roast.

4. Add the water to the pan, cover tightly, and place in a 350-degree-F oven.

5. Roast 2 to 2 1/2 hours until very tender. Check the meat halfway through the process, turn it over, and redistribute the seasonings and vegetables. Reserve the pan drippings.

6. Cool the roast and shred with a fork or by hand.

FOR ROAST

1 chuck roast, approximately 3 1/2 to 4 1/2 pounds

Salt and pepper to taste

1 tablespoon Mexican oregano, toasted (optional)

1 to 2 tablespoons New Mexican, chipotle, or ancho chile powder, lightly toasted, or 4 to 5 fresh jalapeño chiles, sliced in half lengthwise (optional)

2 carrots, peeled and thickly sliced

1 onion, sliced

6 cloves garlic, peeled

6 bay leaves, toasted

4 to 6 sprigs fresh thyme (optional)

2 cups water

FOR FINISHING

2 tablespoons vegetable oil or lard

1/2 onion, sliced in thin strips

3 to 4 roma tomatoes, quartered, seeded, and sliced in 1/4 inch strips

Pan drippings from the roast or Recado de Bistec (see page 199) as needed

Dash of mild vinegar or lime juice

Salt and pepper to taste

OPTIONAL ADDITIONS

Toasted cumin

Toasted Mexican oregano

Poblano Chile Rajas (see page 206)

Chile Caribe

Dried red chiles, toasted, stemmed, and cut into thin strips

Jalapeño or serrano chiles, thinly sliced

Cooked potatoes

Cilantro or parsley, chopped

7. In a preheated heavy skillet, add the oil and sauté the onion until it starts to brown. Add the tomato strips and cook for 1 minute while stirring gently.

8. Add the shredded meat and any optional additions and fry until hot. Add pan drippings or Recado de Bistec and the vinegar or lime juice to moisten to desired consistency. Adjust the seasonings with salt and pepper.

Cabrito Asado Nuevo León
NUEVO LEÓN–STYLE ROASTED YOUNG GOAT

ROASTED, GRILLED, OR SMOKED KID GOAT is popular throughout La Frontera. Available in the markets, from street vendors, and at family gatherings, it makes a great filling for tacos or as the centerpiece of a more formal meal. This version is flavored with orange and comes with a salsa made from beer. Monterey is one of two main locations for breweries in Mexico, so the beer flavor is appropriate. This recipe could also be prepared with young pig, whole pork leg, or leg of lamb.

MAKES 6 SERVINGS

1. Combine the garlic, chile strips, vinegar, and orange juice in a bowl and steep for 20 to 30 minutes. Stir in lard or oil.

2. Spread the pieces of kid, previously cleaned and dried, with the lard and orange juice combined with the garlic mixture; sprinkle with salt. Place on a roasting pan, cover with foil, and place in a preheated oven at 325 degrees F for 2 to 2 1/2 hours or until the meat is tender. Remove foil to allow the meat to brown. (Note: you can prepare this dish using an outdoor grill or smoker with indirect heat. Loosely cover meat with foil to maintain moisture; a pan of water over the heat source also helps.)

3. For the sauce, heat the lard, then sauté the onion until lightly browned; add the chiles, tomatoes, beer, and salt to taste. Boil for 2 to 3 minutes. Remove from heat and add cilantro.

FOR THE MEAT

8 to 10 cloves garlic, peeled and smashed

1 guajillo or New Mexican red chile, toasted, stemmed, seeded, and cut into 1/4-inch strips

2 tablespoons vinegar (cider or pineapple)

Juice of 6 oranges

1 small kid goat (4 to 5 pounds), skinned, cut into pieces, and patted dry

1/4 pound pork lard or cooking oil

3 tablespoons coarse salt

FOR THE SAUCE

1 tablespoon pork lard or vegetable oil

1 white onion, finely chopped

6 serrano chiles, stemmed and thinly sliced

4 tomatoes, seeded and chopped

2/3 cup beer

Salt to taste

1 bunch cilantro, roughly chopped

Durango-Style White Beans

THIS IS ANOTHER SIMPLE yet delicious dish from the ranch that shares roots with Frijoles Charros (see page 53). I included a chipotle chile in the recipe as it complements the ham and bacon.

MAKES 6 TO 8 SERVINGS

1. Cook the beans with garlic, adding salt when cooked through (see page 17).

2. Heat the lard in a saucepan; add the onion and fry until lightly colored.

3. Add the chipotle chile if using, chorizo, ham, and bacon and fry lightly for a few more minutes until the bacon and chorizo are cooked.

4. Add the beans, epazote, and beer and simmer for 20 to 30 minutes. Serve garnished with the pickled chiles and a squeeze of lime or a dash of vinegar and with thick flour tortillas, cheese quesadillas, or crusty bread.

1 pound white beans

2 cloves garlic

Salt to taste

2 tablespoons pork lard

1 medium onion, finely chopped

8 ounces chopped chorizo

8 ounces chopped ham

4 or 5 slices bacon, diced

1 sprig fresh or 1 tablespoon dried epazote

1/2 cup light beer

1 chipotle seco chile, seeded, minced, and toasted (optional)

Pickled chiles and vinegar or lime juice (for garnish)

Thick flour tortillas, cheese quesadillas, or crusty bread (on the side)

Empanadas de Harina
FLOUR PASTRY TURNOVERS

FOR DOUGH

2 1/2 cups whole wheat flour

1 teaspoon baking powder

1 1/2 teaspoons salt

1/8 cup vegetable shortening or lard*

1/3 cup warm water

1 egg, well beaten or 1/4 cup cold water blended with 1 tablespoon flour

Oil for frying

FOR MEAT FILLING
choose one of the following

Carnitas (see page 166)

Machaca Norteña (see page 35)

Pierna de Cerdo Adobada (see page 105)

For sweet empanadas, butter may be substituted for vegetable shortening or lard.

ALTHOUGH CORN REIGNS supreme throughout Mexico, in the North wheat flour is just as important. Empanadas, or turnovers, are filled with a variety of ingredients ranging from savory meat and chile combinations, seafood, vegetables, and cheese to sweet fruit conserves and custards. I prefer to use whole wheat flour for these empanadas, but all-purpose flour works fine. Empanadas can be made large or smaller and bite-sized, in which case they are known as "empanaditas." Traditionally empanadas are fried, but they can also be baked in the oven.

This dough recipe could also be used for flour tortillas if you knead the dough for about 5 minutes extra to develop the gluten and make it a little stretchy.

MAKES 12 TO 14 EMPANADAS OR 25 EMPANADITAS

1. In a bowl, mix the dry ingredients well.

2. With a fork or pastry blender, incorporate the shortening completely into the flour.

3. Add the water, a little at a time, into the flour mixture. Mix well by kneading just until the liquid is well distributed and the dough is smooth and medium-stiff.

4. Gather the dough into a ball and wrap in plastic to maintain the moisture. Allow to rest at room temperature for 30 to 40 minutes (this step is very important).

5. On a well-floured, smooth surface, evenly roll out the dough to approximately 1/8 inch thick. Cut out circles with a pastry cutter, biscuit cutter, or water glass (6 to 7 inches in diameter for empanadas and 3 to 3 1/2 inches for empanaditas).

6. Before filling, brush the outer 1/4-inch edge of each circle with the egg wash or the flour and water mixture.

7. Place the filling in the center of the dough (about 1/4 cup for empanadas and a heaping tablespoon for empanaditas), being careful not to get any of the filling on the moistened edges. Do not overfill.

8. Fold the edges of the dough over to make a half-moon shape and press around the edges to create a seal. You can use a fork to crimp the edges for a more decorative look. The empanadas may be stored (laid out on a baking sheet or other pan and well wrapped in the refrigerator) for several hours before cooking if needed.

9. Fry until golden brown in 365-degree vegetable oil deep enough to cover the empanadas. Drain on paper towels and serve hot. If you wish to bake them instead, brush each empanada with a little egg wash (sprinkle with sugar for the sweet ones) and place them on a baking sheet in a 400-degree oven. Bake until golden brown, about 16 to 18 minutes for small ones and up to 25 minutes for the larger ones.

FOR SEAFOOD FILLING
choose one of the following

Manilla (see page 95)

Camarones Enchipotlados (see page 113)

Pescado Patzcuaro (see page 161)

FOR OTHER FILLING
choose one of the following

Chile Poblano Rajas (see page 206)

Elotes Asados (see page 162)

Frijoles Colados Yucateco (see page 189)

FOR SWEET FILLING
choose one of the following

Fresh or preserved fruit or your favorite pie filling

Pastry cream, sweetened cream, or ricotta cheese

Caldo de Tomate con Albóndigas de Pescado
TOMATO BROTH WITH FISH MEATBALLS

I TASTED THIS REFRESHING SOUP at a food vendor in the market in La Paz, Baja California. The vendor was not forthcoming with the recipe, but I have been able to reconstruct it with the help of several of my Mexican friends and a bit of experimentation. For a main course, you may want to serve it in a bowl with a portion of Arroz a la Poblana (see page 133) or saffron rice.

MAKES 6 TO 8 SERVINGS

1. In a saucepan, boil the water with the onion, herbs, salt, peppercorns, and cloves for 5 minutes. Squeeze the lime or lemon in the water then add to the water.

2. Place the fish in the water and boil for 5 more minutes.

3. Remove the fish and pat dry. Strain the cooking broth and reserve in the refrigerator.

4. Fry the fish in the oil until slightly browned. Cool, remove the skin and any bones, and finely chop.

5. In a bowl, mix the fish with the bread or cracker crumbs, flour, and eggs and let sit for 10 to 15 minutes.

6. Form into small, bite-size balls and refrigerate until ready to use.

   Note: If the fish balls are too dry, just add a little of the reserved cooking liquid to moisten.

FISH MEATBALLS

6 cups water

1/2 white onion, roughly chopped

1 sprig each fresh marjoram, thyme, and oregano or 1 tablespoon toasted Mexican oregano

2 bay leaves, toasted

1 teaspoon salt

6 whole black peppercorns

6 whole cloves

1/2 lime or lemon

1 1/2 pounds white fish, whole or fillets, skin on if possible

2 tablespoons vegetable oil

2/3 cup bread or cracker crumbs, or 1/3 cup masa harina

1/3 cup all-purpose flour

2 eggs, well beaten

TOMATO BROTH

1/2 white onion, sliced into thin strips

1 chile chipotle seco, or 1 chipotle chile en adobe, or 1 to 2 chiles serrano cut 1/2 inch lengthwise

3 cloves garlic, sliced

2 tablespoons vegetable oil

1 pound ripe tomatoes, charred, pureed, and strained

Reserved fish cooking broth or Caldo de Pescado

1 sprig fresh epazote (optional)

Salt and pepper to taste

Fresh cilantro and lime (for garnish)

7. For broth, fry the onion, chile, and garlic in the oil until lightly browned.

8. Add the tomato puree and fry for 1 to 2 minutes more.

9. Add the fish broth and epazote and lower the heat to a slow boil and cook for 10 minutes. Taste and season with salt and pepper.

10. Carefully add the fish meatballs and simmer for about 10 more minutes until the meatballs are well heated. Remove the chiles and epazote if you like.

11. Garnish with cilantro and lime and serve.

Jocoque
MEXICAN-STYLE SOUR CREAM

THE RICH GRAZING LANDS around Monterrey produce some of the richest cream in Mexico. This is a homemade version of sour cream. Its nutty, rich sourness is more akin to the French crème fraiche than the commercial sour cream varieties available in the United States. In Mexico, the homemade jocoque is usually cultured from the previous batch; it ranges in consistency from pourable, like heavy cream, to thick and custard-like. Once you make the first batch, you may continue the culture by adding some of the previous batch to fresh cream to produce more. Jocoque is a great garnish for many Mexican plates.

MAKES 1 + QUARTS

1. Place the cream and the buttermilk in a stainless steel or glass container and mix well.

2. Leave uncovered for 1 to 2 hours at room temperature.

3. Cover tightly and leave in a warm place (78 to 90 degrees is ideal) for 12 to 24 hours. The top of the refrigerator or a high kitchen shelf works well.

4. Add the lime juice and salt. Cover again and refrigerate until well chilled. The jocoque should thicken after several hours. If it becomes too thick, you may add milk to thin to the desired consistency. Store covered in the refrigerator.

*1 quart light whipping cream**

1/8 cup buttermilk or jocoque from the previous batch

1 tablespoon fresh lime juice (optional)

Pinch of salt

If you can find cream that is not ultra-pasteurized, it will culture faster.

Tacos de Pescado
BAJA-STYLE FISH TACOS

RUBIO'S BAJA GRILL in San Diego started the fish taco craze north of the border in 1983 when Ralph Rubio transplanted his favorite recipe from a small taco vendor on the Baja coast to his southern California restaurant. Here is my version of this beachside treat. It borrows from the English fish and chips, but is very much like the tacos served beachside in Baja, California. The dredging and the second round of frying are the secret to crispy fish.

MAKES 18 SERVINGS

1. Mix half of the beer with all other ingredients except fish, oil, and tortillas; blend well with a whisk.

2. When all lumps have been smoothed, continue to add remaining beer until a batter with a consistency slightly thinner than pancake batter is attained. Keep the batter chilled.

3. Dredge fish filets in flour and dip in batter, being careful to coat completely. Allow excess to drip back into the batter.

4. Fry the fish in 350-degree oil for 2 1/2 to 4 minutes until golden brown and cooked through. Drain well and allow to cool slightly.

5. When ready to serve, heat tortillas and place in a towel or cloth to keep warm.

6. Refry the fish for about 1 more minute to make it crispy.

7. Place fish in warm tortillas and garnish with shredded cabbage and salsa; mayonnaise; sour cream flavored with chipotle chiles en adobo; or chopped, pickled jalapeño, cilantro, and lime juice.

1 1/2 pounds Dorado (mahi-mahi) or other firm fish, cut in 2 1/2-inch pieces

8 ounces full-flavored pale ale or Mexican lager

3 whole eggs, well beaten

2 teaspoons Coleman's dry mustard (optional)

1 teaspoon onion powder (optional)

1 teaspoon ground chipotle chile or other red chile powder (optional)

1 tablespoon salt

Pepper to taste

2 teaspoons sugar

1 1/2 cups all-purpose flour + 1 cup for dredging

Oil for frying (preferably canola or peanut oil)

Flour or corn tortillas

Caldo de Habas con Nopales
FAVA BEAN SOUP WITH CACTUS

FAVA BEANS ARE AN OLD-WORLD INGREDIENT. The beans are enjoyed in Mexico especially during Lent when eating meat is restricted. In Sonora, where I learned this recipe, prickly pear cactus is added to make a more hearty and healthy soup. The use of meat broth in the preparation adds extra depth of flavor.

MAKES 8 TO 10 SERVINGS

1. Cook the fava beans in enough unsalted water to cover (1 inch deeper than the beans) until the beans are soft and cooked through completely, about 1-1/4 hours or 25 to 30 minutes in a pressure cooker. Drain.

2. Blend the chiles, tomatoes, onion, and garlic with half the water or broth; strain and fry in the olive oil for 1 to 2 minutes.

3. Add the remaining liquid and the favas and simmer for 20 to 30 minutes.

4. Add the baked prickly pear cactus, cilantro, salt and pepper and simmer 5 more minutes. Garnish with crumbled cheese, drops of olive oil, and more cilantro or mint.

2 1/2 cups dry yellow fava beans, peeled and lightly toasted

3 to 4 chiles guajillos, stemmed, seeded, soaked, and toasted

6 to 8 plum tomatoes, charred

4 cloves garlic, comal-roasted until slightly blackened in spots then peeled

1 1/2 quarts water or Caldo de Res or Pollo (see pages 140, 138)

2 to 3 tablespoons olive oil

1 1/4 pounds prickly pear cactus paddles, cleaned, cut into strips, tossed with olive oil, and baked until lightly browned (about 20 minutes at 400 degrees F)

1/3 cup roughly chopped cilantro (mint may be substituted, all or in part)

2 teaspoons salt

Black pepper to taste

1 medium white onion, peeled, thickly sliced, and roasted on a comal or griddle until well browned

Crumbled cheese, olive oil, cilantro, or mint (for garnish)

Churros

5 cups water

1 cup butter

2 teaspoons salt

1/2 cup sugar

1/2 cup corn, soy, or canola oil

1 teaspoon ground allspice or cloves

5 cups all-purpose flour

2 teaspoons Mexican vanilla extract

8 eggs

2 cups corn, soy, canola,
  or peanut oil

Cinnamon sugar (1 part cinnamon
  to 3 parts sugar)

*Note: Serve with hot chocolate or
  tempered chocolate with Helado de
  Coco on the side.

CHURROS, one of my favorite street snacks, originated in Spain and are still popular there. Churros have all of the qualities of a fresh doughnut or beignet with a little extra crunch. Churros are fairly easy to prepare but can be a little messy to make until you get the hang of it.

MAKES ABOUT 2 DOZEN 3-INCH CHURROS

1. Heat water, butter, salt, sugar, 1/2 cup oil, and allspice or cloves to a rolling boil.

2. Stir in flour, stirring vigorously over low heat until mixture forms a ball (about 1 minute).

3. Remove from heat. Add vanilla extract. Beat eggs in one at a time. Continue beating until smooth (about 30 seconds).

4. Let the dough cool.

5. Place dough in a piping bag or cookie press fitted with a large star tip.

6. In a large frying pan, heat 2 cups oil to 360 degrees F.

7. Pipe the churros in long rods, 3 to 4 inches, directly into the hot oil. Fry until golden brown on all sides. Place on paper towels to drain.

8. Dust with cinnamon sugar and serve with hot chocolate. Churros may also be dipped in tempered chocolate and cooled for a decadent garnish with Helado de Coco (see page 101).

Chiles Jalapeños en Escabeche
PICKLED JALAPEÑO CHILES

ALTHOUGH THE STATE OF VERACRUZ is well known for its jalapeño chiles, I have placed this recipe in the La Frontera section in honor of my many Chihuahuense amigos. In the north of Mexico, many food items are dried or pickled to preserve them, and pickled jalapeños are as popular here as in any other part of the country. This method is easy, produces tasty chiles, and may be adapted to home canning for a bumper crop from the garden. Without canning, the chiles will keep in the fridge for several months. They are versatile and may be used for salsas or garnishes, or simply as a snack. You may also use other chiles such as serrano or yellow hots.

1. Place all ingredients except the chiles and the water in a nonreactive pot and heat to boiling.

2. Remove from the heat and add the cool water.

3. Stir in the chiles and allow to cool to room temperature.

4. Place in a glass or other nonreactive container, seal well, and refrigerate for 48 hours.

5. Stir well, taste, and add additional salt if needed.

6. Store tightly covered in the refrigerator.

1 white onion, peeled and quartered

1 carrot, peeled and sliced

6 cloves garlic, peeled

5 bay leaves, toasted

1 teaspoon coriander seeds, toasted

1 teaspoon whole black pepper, lightly toasted

2 sprigs oregano or 1 tablespoon toasted Mexican oregano

2 sprigs thyme or 1 tablespoon dried thyme

3 tablespoons kosher or sea salt

1/3 cup sugar

1 quart apple cider vinegar

1 pint distilled white vinegar

1 cup cool water

1 pound whole fresh jalapeño chiles (about 18 depending on size), rinsed well and dried

Caldillo Norteño
DURANGO-STYLE BEEF STEW

1 pound ripe tomatoes

2 cloves garlic

1 medium white onion

4 tablespoons vegetable oil

2 cups diced potatoes

1 cup diced carrots

1 teaspoon Mexican oregano,
   toasted

Salt and pepper to taste

2 1/2 pounds beef chuck, diced in
   1/2-inch cubes or 16 ounces beef
   jerky broken into 1/2-inch pieces

3 tablespoons vegetable oil

2 tablespoons all-purpose flour
   (optional)

2 quarts Caldo de Res (see page
   140) (water may be used but the
   stew won't be as rich)

12 chiles pasados (dry green chiles),
   rehydrated in water and finely
   chopped or 1/2 cup roasted,
   peeled, and finely chopped New
   Mexico green chiles

4 Chiles Poblano Rajas (see page
   206)

A SIMPLE STEW originally made with dry chiles and dried beef, Caldillo Norteño is representative of the simple but hearty foods of the cattle-producing state of Durango. The addition of a cup or two of fresh sweet corn makes a tasty variation.

MAKES 8 TO 10 SERVINGS

1. In a blender, puree the tomato with the garlic and onion; strain.

2. Heat the oil in a saucepan, then add the potatoes and carrots. Sauté on high for 1 or 2 minutes, and then add the blended vegetables, oregano, salt, and pepper. Sauté 1 more minute. Remove from heat.

3. Fry the beef in oil until well browned and add the vegetable mixture.* Continue stirring for 1 or 2 minutes, then add the Caldo de Res and the chiles pasados. Simmer gently for 45 minutes to 1 hour or until the meat is tender.

4. Add the chiles poblanos and simmer 5 more minutes. Serve very hot.

*If you prefer a little thicker broth in your stew, you may dredge the beef with 2 tablespoons all-purpose flour before frying in the oil.

Frijoles Charros
COWBOY-STYLE BEANS

FRIJOLES CHARROS OR "COWBOY BEANS" are served throughout Mexico. This version comes from the highlands around Guadalajara, the home of the original "charros," consummate horsemen and lasso artists who wear the formal clothing and large hats associated with Mariachi. My first taste of this rustic dish was on the island of Cozumel in Quintana Roo where it is made with chorizo, chunks of pork, and slices of salchicha (a hot dog–type meat that resembles Vienna sausage). This makes a great side dish, a main dish for lunch with tortillas, or a light supper along with your favorite tacos.

MAKES 8 TO 10 SERVINGS

1. Cook the chorizo and the bacon over medium heat until the fat is rendered. Pour off half of the fat.

2. Continue cooking and add the onion and garlic. Cook until translucent, and then add the oregano, cumin, ancho chile, bay leaves, and chipotle.

3. Add salt, beans, vinegar, and broth. Simmer on low for 45 minutes to 1 hour. Add the epazote about halfway through this step.

4. Garnish with your choice of chopped onions, radishes, shredded cabbage, lime wedges, crumbled cheese, and cilantro or toasted oregano, and serve with fresh flour or corn tortillas.

6 ounces uncooked Mexican chorizo or hot Italian sausage (casings removed), crumbled

3 slices smoked bacon, diced

1 medium white onion, chopped

2 cloves garlic, crushed

1 teaspoon toasted dried Mexican oregano (see page 25)

1/2 teaspoon toasted ground cumin seed

1 ancho chile, toasted, stemmed, and seeded, then crumbled

2 bay leaves, toasted

1 teaspoon pureed chipotle chile en adobo

1 teaspoon salt

3 1/2 cups cooked pinto beans (see page 17)

1 teaspoon apple cider vinegar

1 1/2 cups rich chicken or pork broth

1 whole sprig fresh epazote or 1 tablespoon dried epazote

La Costa Oro

LA COSTA DEL ORO, THE GOLD COAST, RUNS ALONG THE PACIFIC
Ocean from Mazatlán in the north to sunny Acapulco in the south. Other well-known resorts in this region include Puerto Vallarta, Manzanillo, and Zihuatanejo. In addition to the coastline areas, the foothills of the Sierra Madre Mountains and adjacent inland regions also make up this area. La Costa del Oro is known for its incredible diversity of seafood, abundant tropical fruits, pork and wild game, and last but definitely not least, its tequila.

Along with its own indigenous roots, the region exhibits many historical influences from Spain, England, and France. Contemporary foods in La Costa Oro reflect the many fiestas celebrated in Mexico. Indeed, traditional Mexican fare has prevailed. If you are adventurous, you may try various insects, larvae, worms, unusual beverages, parrot soup, and iguana tamales, among many other exotic regional foods. However, many selections suit a more conservative palate. The pozole of Guerrero, bread soup of Colima, shrimp tamales of Nayarit, churipo of Michoacán, and char-grilled whole fish from Sinaloa will surely satisfy your cravings.

Al Pastor

PORK COOKED WITH PINEAPPLES AND CHILES

3 to 3 1/2 pounds boneless pork loin or stew meat cut into bite-sized chunks

Salt and pepper

2 cups of fresh diced pineapple, reserving any juice

1/2 white onion, diced

10 cloves garlic, coarsely chopped

4 to 6 ancho chiles, toasted, stemmed, seeded, soaked (see page 25), then pureed

2 guajillo or chipotle seco chiles, toasted, stemmed, seeded, soaked (see page 25), then pureed (optional)

3 to 4 roma tomatoes, well charred and pureed

2 to 3 cups of water and reserved pineapple juice

2 tablespoons vinegar (pineapple, apple cider, or rice)

1 teaspoon whole or 1/2 teaspoon ground cloves

1 stick canela (optional)

THE TERM *AL PASTOR* loosely translated means "cooked shepherd's style." This dish originally may have been prepared with mutton or lamb, but these days in Mexico *al pastor* refers to pork that is usually used in tacos. The typical commercial method of cooking this recipe involves slow-roasting pieces of meat layered on a rotisserie spit with fresh pineapple to combine the flavors. The meat is then sliced off the spit. Along the Gold Coast in Jalisco and Nayarit, the small, sweet, local pineapples are the perfect contrast to the rich pork and zesty chiles. I have created a homecooked version that is a stew and may be more like the original recipe. It can be used as a taco or chile relleno filling or as a tasty main course.

MAKES 6 TO 8 SERVINGS

1. Season the meat with salt and pepper; mix with the pineapple chunks and marinate for at least 2 hours or overnight. (If you are substituting canned pineapple for fresh pineapple, reduce marinating time to 30 to 60 minutes.)

2. Preheat a heavy skillet or casserole over high heat, add the pork, and sear until well browned on all sides. Add the onion and garlic and cook 1 more minute.

3. With the skillet still on high, add the chile and tomato purees and fry for 1 to 2 minutes more.

4. Add enough water and juice to just cover the meat. Add the vinegar and cloves, and cinnamon and achiote paste if using. Stir well to combine the seasonings, then cover and simmer for 30 to 45 minutes (or bake in an oven at 350 degrees F), stirring occasionally and adding water as needed to prevent burning. Only add just enough liquid to allow cooking, since the dish is better if slightly dry.

5. When the meat is tender, uncover the pot and cook until almost all of the liquid is absorbed.

1 tablespoon achiote paste or Recado Colorado (see page 197) (optional)

1 tablespoon vegetable oil (for spit-roasted method only)

CLASSIC SPIT-ROASTED METHOD

If you have a rotisserie, you may approximate the classic spit-roasted method by doing the following:

1. Use boneless pork loin chops and slice the pineapple.

2. Stack the pork chops, alternating every third chop with a pineapple slice, and then skewer with the rotisserie spit.

3. Prepare the sauce as stated on the previous page, but with the following exceptions: do not use the meat and only simmer for 5 minutes, do not use the canela, and add 1 tablespoon vegetable oil to the tomato puree.

4. Liberally brush the skewered meat with the sauce and marinate for 30 minutes.

5. Place the spit over a charcoal or gas grill and cook slowly, constantly rotating and brushing with more sauce every few minutes until meat is well browned and tender.

6. Allow the meat to rest a few minutes and then carve thin slices off with a sharp knife.

7. Serve with corn tortillas and garnish with chopped onions, cilantro, and slices of lime.

Ceviche

CITRUS-MARINATED FRESH FISH

REPORTEDLY ORIGINATING IN PERU, ceviche is served throughout Latin America in many forms: with fish, scallops, or shrimp; with or without chiles; and with a variety of vegetables, herbs, and citrus fruit. Almost all versions contain onions; in fact, the word *ceviche* is derived from the Spanish for onion—*cebolla*. The process of marinating in an acid-like lime juice actually "cooks" the raw seafood through oxidation rather than through the use of heat. It is essential to use only the freshest, highest quality seafood in this preparation. Ceviche should be consumed as soon as it is ready; it doesn't keep well like escabeche and the texture can get very chewy, so don't make it more than an hour or so ahead of time.

MAKES 6 TO 8 APPETIZERS OR 4 MAIN COURSE SALADS

1. If you are using fish, cut into bite-sized or smaller pieces. Shellfish should be peeled, shelled, and either left whole or cut into smaller pieces.

2. Combine everything except the tomato and optional ingredients in a nonreactive container. Cover container and chill. Marinate for 30 minutes to 2 hours (but no more than 2 hours because the seafood will begin to toughen).

3. Mix in whatever optional ingredients you are using. Wait 5 minutes, stir again, and taste. Adjust the seasoning and serve as soon as possible.

2 pounds fresh, skinless fish fillets, bay scallops, shrimp, or a mix of all three

1 large or 2 medium red onions, rinsed and finely diced (see page 19)

2 jalapeño or serrano chiles, stemmed, seeded, and minced

1/4 cup fresh lime juice

2 tablespoons fresh orange or grapefruit juice

1 teaspoon vinegar (apple cider, pineapple, or rice)

1 teaspoon orange, lime, or grapefruit zest, very finely minced (optional)

1 teaspoon salt

1/2 teaspoon sugar or honey

3/4 cup peeled, seeded, and diced cucumber (optional)

3 to 4 small ripe tomatoes or 1 red sweet bell pepper, seeded and diced

1/4 cup chopped cilantro or flat-leafed parsley

1 tablespoon olive oil (optional)

Jicama, diced (optional)

Coconut milk and/or shredded unsweetened coconut (optional)

Melon, diced (optional)

Pineapple, diced (optional)

Capers (optional)

Olives, chopped (optional)

59

BREAD SOUP

THIS IS A *SOPA SECA* OR DRY SOUP (not really dry, just not brothy; more of a casserole) that shows the influence of Mediterranean cooking on early Mexican kitchens. Colima, where this recipe is from, is somewhat isolated and has retained that colonial influence for centuries. I would not be opposed to the addition of roasted mild chiles like Poblano, New Mexico green, or Anaheim. The soup makes a hearty supper.

This recipe involves a lot of different steps using a number of different ingredients. To make it a little more simple, you may want to prepare the hen, the sauce, and the filling in advance of assembling and cooking the bread soup. If the ingredients are cold when assembled, just add another 10 to 12 minutes of cooking time.

SERVES 10 TO 12

1. To prepare the sauce, blend and strain the tomatoes and onion, then fry in the oil used to cook the chorizo sausage until thickened like spaghetti sauce.

2. Add the strained chicken broth, coriander, cumin, canela, and orange juice. Simmer 10 minutes to allow the flavors to develop.

3. To prepare the filling, first shred the cooked chicken.

4. Fry the slices of bread in the hot lard or oil until golden brown on both sides and leave to drain on paper towels.

5. Lightly fry corn tortillas in oil or lard, and line the bottom of a large casserole dish with them. This will prevent the soup from sticking. Place a layer of bread on the tortillas, followed by a layer

FOR THE SAUCE

7 tomatoes, roasted

1 large onion

1 1/2 quarts strained broth from cooking the chicken or Caldo de Pollo

1 1/2 teaspoons toasted coriander seeds, ground

Pinch of toasted, ground cumin

2 sticks canela

1/2 cup juice of a Seville orange (or 1/8 cup lime juice and 3/8 cup orange juice with a dash of cider vinegar)

FOR THE HEN

1 stewing hen cut into pieces and cooked in enough water to cover along with:

2 onions, peeled and cut in half

1 tablespoon Mexican oregano, toasted

6 cloves garlic, peeled

2 carrots, peeled and thickly sliced

3 sticks celery, thickly sliced

3 bay leaves, toasted

6 whole peppercorns

Salt to taste

61

FOR THE BREAD

10 corn tortillas

1/2 cup lard or 1/2 cup vegetable oil or a combination

1 pound crusty bread cut in 1/2-inch-thick slices

FOR THE FILLING

12 ounces loose chorizo, fried in a little oil and crumbled

2 carrots, peeled, boiled, and sliced

2 to 3 potatoes, boiled, peeled, and sliced

1 cup green beans, blanched and sliced

3/4 cup fresh or frozen peas

4 eggs, boiled for 12 minutes, cooled, peeled, and sliced

2 firm plantains, peeled, sliced, and fried golden brown

3/4 cup assorted lightly blanched vegetables (squash, corn, broccoli, cauliflower, chiles, etc.)

3/4 cup pitted green olives

1/2 cup slivered almonds, lightly toasted

2/3 cup raisins, soaked in 1/3 cup sweet sherry or fruit juice

of the shredded chicken, then a layer of each of the filling ingredients, and end with a layer of bread. (Reserve a few almonds and slices of plantain and egg for garnish.)

6. Pour a generous amount of tomato broth over the filling, and place in the oven at 350 degrees for 40 minutes or until very hot and lightly browned, but not dry.

7. Garnish with almonds and slices of plantain and egg.

Tepache
FERMENTED PINEAPPLE BEVERAGE

I FIRST ENCOUNTERED THIS DRINK in the Mercado in Xalapa, Veracruz, and it was like nothing I had tasted before. It was cool and refreshing, slightly sweet and fruity, with a little spritz of carbonation and a hint of alcohol. Easy to make if you have a container and the space to keep it, tepache is a perfect beverage for a summertime outdoor fiesta. The process for making it is a lot like making pineapple vinegar. Tepache is purported to have originated in Mexico State; however, it is widely available, and because of the great pineapples grown in la Costa del Oro, I have included the recipe here.

MAKES 7 QUARTS

2 medium ripe pineapples, at least 3 pounds total

1 3/4 pounds piloncillo or light brown sugar

1 1/2 gallons water

2 sticks cinnamon

4 to 5 whole cloves (optional)

1 12-ounce bottle of beer (optional) Bottle-conditioned ales with live yeast work best, but any beer that is not too dark will do.

1. Cut the tops off the pineapples, leaving the skin on. Rinse well and cut into eighths lengthwise.

2. If using piloncillo, heat with 1 cup of the water until dissolved. Cool.

3. Place the pineapple, piloncillo water or sugar, cinnamon, and cloves (if using) in a glass or nonreactive metal container with 1 gallon of the water. Mix well to dissolve the sugar.

4. Leave uncovered for 2 hours, then cover (not too tightly), and let sit for 48 to 72 hours at room temperature.

5. Strain the liquid and return to the container. Add the rest of the water and the beer, if using.

6. Cover and let sit for 24 to 48 hours more.

7. Taste and add more water or beer to achieve desired sweetness. The tepache should be a little carbonated and sweet but not cloyingly so.

8. Refrigerate to store and serve cold.

Pollo a las Brasas (Asados)

CHARCOAL-GRILLED CHICKEN ON A STICK

A SIMPLE WAY TO COOK CHICKEN over the coals outdoors, Pollo a las Brasas uses sticks or large skewers to control the distance of the chicken from the heat. This version is from Sinaloa on the Pacific Coast in northwest Mexico and uses citrus, chiles, garlic, and spices as a marinade. Originally cooked over an open fire, this dish can also be made using a grill, smoker, rotisserie, or indoor oven. The sticks are optional. Pollo a las Brasas accompanied by Salsa Fresca (see page 143), white rice, some charred jalapeño or poblano chiles, and fresh lime, avocado, and homemade flour tortillas is a combination relished throughout the country.

MAKES 4 TO 8 SERVINGS

1. Rinse the chickens and pat dry. Arrange in a nonreactive pan and season with the salt and pepper.

2. Combine the remaining ingredients and cover the chicken with the mixture.

3. Cover the pan and refrigerate for at least 2 hours and up to 12 hours.

4. Remove from the refrigerator 1/2 hour before cooking. Skewer if desired.

5. Cook over a low-heat charcoal fire or indirect heat in a covered grill or smoker, turning frequently (every 7 to 10 minutes), until chicken is cooked through (approximately 1 to 1 1/2 hours).

4 half chickens
   (1 to 1 1/4 pound each)

2 teaspoons salt

1 teaspoon ground black pepper

4 guajillo chiles, toasted, seeded, and
   finely chopped or ground

12 cloves garlic

1 teaspoon whole toasted cumin

1 tablespoon fresh rosemary leaves,
   chopped, or 1 tablespoon toasted
   Mexican oregano

2 sticks cinnamon, lightly crushed
   (optional)

2 teaspoons whole allspice, lightly
   cracked (optional)

2/3 cup fresh lime juice

1/4 cup vegetable oil

Tamales de Camarón Nayarit
NAYARIT-STYLE SHRIMP TAMALES

FOR THE TAMALES

4 cups shrimp broth (made from
  shrimp shells or by adding 2
  tablespoons ground dried
  shrimp to hot water), or Caldo
  de Pescado, or Caldo de Pollo
  (see pages 141, 138)

4 cups masa harina

1 teaspoon salt

6 ounces pork lard, or 4 ounces
  softened butter and 2 ounces
  vegetable shortening

Water as needed

Banana leaves to make 24 to 30
  tamale wrappers* (plus a little
  extra to make ties)

*24 to 30 large cornhusks, well
  soaked, may be used instead

FOR THE FILLING

3 pounds raw shrimp, peeled and
  deveined

1 1/2 pounds tomatillos, husked,
  rinsed, and roasted on a comal
  or heavy skillet until lightly
  browned

ALL ALONG THE PACIFIC COAST OF MEXICO, seafood is cooked in tamales. In the state of Nayarit, the shrimp tamales are the most famous. They may be prepared using either fresh shrimp or dried shrimp and come spiced with a variety of different seasonings. This version uses fresh shrimp and is cooked over a charcoal or wood fire, although tamales may also be prepared using a traditional steaming method.

MAKES 24 TO 30 TAMALES

1. Heat the shrimp broth or alternate liquid to a boil and mix well with the masa harina and salt. Cover and set aside to cool.

2. With a mixer, whip the lard or butter and shortening until fluffy. Add small pieces of the masa mix and continue beating, making more additions until all of the masa is incorporated. Add small amounts of cool water as needed to maintain a moist batter. (The finished masa should be fairly moist, yet thick enough that when a spoonful is inverted it remains in the spoon.) Continue whipping on high speed until a small piece of the prepared tamale masa floats in a cup of cold water. Set aside in a cool place.

3. Blend all of the filling ingredients together, except the shrimp. Then mix in the shrimp.

4. Toast the banana leaves to make them pliable (see page 29).

5. Place a banana leaf (or cornhusk if using) on a flat surface, shiny-side-up, and spread enough masa in the center to make a 5 x 5-inch square about 1/4 to 3/8 inch thick. Place about 2 tablespoons of the shrimp filling in the center of the masa and fold the leaf to make a

package that is well sealed. Tie with strips of the leaf to secure. Repeat until all of the filling is used.

6. Place the tamales on the grate of a charcoal, wood, or gas grill and cook over a low or indirect heat. (You might want to use a piece of foil, turned shiny-side-down, under the tamales if you have trouble controlling the heat. Another piece of foil or banana leaf loosely placed over the tamales can help to retain the moisture and speed up the cooking process.) Turn the tamales every 10 to 15 minutes to cook evenly. It usually takes about 40 to 60 minutes to cook through.

Note: Tamales may also be cooked in a steamer for 60 to 75 minutes.

1 large white onion, peeled, thickly sliced, and pan-roasted until slightly blackened (see page 23)

4 cloves garlic, pan-roasted until slightly blackened (see page 23)

4 to 5 guajillo chiles or 10 to 12 chiles de arbol, toasted, stemmed, seeded, and soaked (see page 25)*

2 tablespoons fresh oregano or cilantro leaves

1 cup pineapple juice

1 1/2 teaspoons salt

*Ancho chiles or California red chiles may be substituted for a milder flavor.

Guacamole

FORMERLY AN EXOTIC MENU SELECTION in the United States, guacamole is now a common dish around the world. Many variations with numerous additions are available, but I prefer this simple, chunky version. Uruapan in western Michoacán is famous throughout Mexico for its delicious avocados. Many Mexican recipes call for *aguacates de Uruapan, como mantequilla* (avocados from Uruapan, like butter). Indeed, a perfectly ripe avocado is creamy, somewhat like butter. Many north-of-the-border recipes call for the addition of lime juice. I enjoy the taste of lime with guacamole, but it should be added just before eating. Contrary to conventional wisdom, the lime juice actually promotes browning.

MAKES 2 1/2 TO 3 CUPS

3 large (or 4 to 5 medium) avocados, peeled and pitted

1/4 cup diced ripe tomato

1 or 2 jalapeño chiles, stemmed, seeded, and finely diced

1/2 red or white onion, rinsed, and finely diced (see page 19)

1/4 teaspoon finely minced garlic (optional)

Tiny pinch of ground cumin (optional)

1/4 cup cilantro leaves, chopped (optional)

Salt to taste

1. Smash the avocados in a bowl or molcajete with a bean masher or with your hands until mostly smooth with a few small chunks remaining. (You get the best texture when you use a molcajete; however, it is harder to clean.)

2. Add the tomato, chiles, and onion. Add the garlic, cumin, and cilantro if using. Mix well and season with salt. You may want to smash some of the tomatoes, onions, and chiles for flavor.

3. Wait 5 to 10 minutes for flavors to develop before serving. Guacamole may be stored for a few hours by covering the surface with plastic wrap and chilling, but it does not do well for extended periods.

4. Serve with lime wedges and crumbly sharp cheese, such as cotija, for garnish.

Vinagre de Piña
PINEAPPLE VINEGAR

THIS MILD VINEGAR is perfect to complement many Mexican dishes. It emulates the fruit vinegars made from leftover and overripe fruit in the homes and markets of Mexico. It is simple to prepare, requiring only time and space, but no special skills. A gallon may seem like a lot to many home cooks but since this vinegar is fairly mild, you will use more of it. You may also experiment with other fruits such as ripe bananas, mangoes, papayas, or apples. Be sure to include the skins.

1 large ripe pineapple

1 gallon water

1 cup natural (not distilled) apple cider vinegar (optional)

1. Thoroughly rinse the pineapple and remove the top.

2. Slice into 1-inch-thick rounds with the skin on.

3. Place in a glass or other nonreactive container with a loose-fitting lid.

4. Cover with water and apple cider vinegar, if using.

5. Cover the container and allow to stand in a warm place (72 to 85 degrees F) for 5 to 7 days. (It only needs to stand 3 to 4 days if using vinegar as a starter.) Taste to ensure the vinegar has cultured; if not, you can leave it a few more days to develop.

6. Strain and store the vinegar in airtight containers.

Sopa de Flor de Calabaza
SQUASH BLOSSOM AND SWEET CORN SOUP

3 scallions or green onions, finely chopped

1 cup zucchini or yellow squash, diced in 1/4-inch cubes

3 tablespoons butter

3 ears fresh sweet corn, roasted in a hot oven or on a char grill, and stripped from the cob*

2 large poblano, Anaheim, or New Mexican green chiles, charred, peeled, seeded (see page 21) and cut into 1/4-inch strips

2 1/2 cups fresh squash blossoms, pistils and stems removed, and cut into 1/2-inch pieces

3 cloves garlic, roasted, peeled, and thinly sliced (see page 23)

2 tablespoons fresh epazote leaves, finely chopped, or 1 tablespoon chopped fresh marjoram

2 1/2 quarts chicken or vegetable broth

Salt to taste

*2 1/2 cups of frozen corn may be substituted

THIS DELICATELY FLAVORED SOUP is prepared throughout Mexico in many variations. During the summer rainy season, it frequently contains huitlacoche, a deeply flavored, dark, mushroom-like corn fungus often referred to as the truffles of Mexico. The canned huitlacoche, while fairly flavorful, imparts a black color to the soup that I prefer to avoid. Sometimes I add some shiitake, chanterelle, morel, or crimini mushrooms that have been separately sautéed at a high temperature after the squash blossoms are cooked. Another interesting substitute is a few drops of white truffle oil as a garnish just before serving. In the highlands of Jalisco (the home of tequila and where this recipe originated), the soup is finished with Jocoque, a naturally soured cream (see page 45), somewhat like crème fraiche.

MAKES 6 TO 8 SERVINGS

1. Sauté the scallions or green onions and zucchini or yellow squash in butter for 2 to 3 minutes until the scallions are tender.

2. Add the corn and chiles and cook for 2 more minutes.

3. Add the squash blossoms, roasted garlic slices, and epazote leaves and cook for 1 additional minute.

4. Add the broth and bring to a boil. Reduce heat and simmer for 15 to 20 minutes.

5. Add salt to taste.

6. Serve in bowls and garnish with tortilla strips, jocoque, and a squeeze of lime.

Camarones en el Mojo de Ajo
GARLIC SHRIMP WITH CHILES

THIS IS A DISH with Spanish-Portuguese roots that benefits from the addition of Mexican chiles. I tasted this version in Sinaloa around Mazatlán where one of the world's largest shrimp-processing plants is located. Fresh is definitely better, but a good-quality frozen shrimp will work also. Make sure the pan is very hot to cook the shrimp quickly. I have given several chile options to suit your taste or availability of ingredients. This dish goes well with Arroz a la Poblana (white rice) (see page 133). ¡Buen Provecho!

MAKES 6 TO 8 SERVINGS

1. Devein the shrimp, either by slicing through the shells to remove the vein or by first peeling, then slicing to devein. Leaving the shell on during the cooking process helps retain moisture and adds to the flavor; however, the shrimp are messier to eat. The tails may also be left on for presentation and to make the shrimp easier to eat with your fingers.

2. Preheat a skillet or sauté pan on medium-high to high heat.

3. Add the oil and/or butter, then the salt, garlic slices, and chiles.

4. Stir vigorously for a few seconds (be careful to only darken, not burn, the chiles), and then turn heat to the highest setting and add the shrimp. Stir occasionally but not too often and cook until the shrimp have turned almost completely pink.

5. Add the liquid and stir. Remove from heat and add the cilantro or parsley. Serve immediately.

2 1/2 to 3 pounds shrimp (any size of shrimp is ok, but larger shrimp are easier to keep from overcooking)

About 1/4 cup olive oil, butter, or a combination of the two

1 to 2 teaspoons salt

8 to 10 cloves garlic, peeled and thinly sliced

1 or 2 ancho or guajillo chiles, toasted, stemmed, seeded (see page 25) and cut crosswise into thin strips

1 to 2 tablespoons chiles de árbol, pequin, chiltepin, or japonés, toasted, seeded, and coarsely chopped (optional, for hotter version)

Juice of 2 limes

1/4 cup chopped cilantro or flat-leafed parsley

El Istmo

TABASCO, OAXACA, AND VERACRUZ

EL ISTMO, THE ISTHMUS, refers to the narrow part of the funnel-shaped neck of land—made up of the states of Oaxaca, Tabasco, and Veracruz—that separates mainland Mexico from the Yucatán peninsula as well as Guatemala and Belize to the southeast. Bounded by the Gulf of Mexico to the north and the Pacific Ocean to the west and south, the landscape ranges from lush tropical wetlands and forests to incredibly tall volcanic mountains, with a fair amount of desert terrain thrown in to lend a certain balance to it all.

To lump all of these areas together as I have is not completely fair; each state could easily be a region unto itself. To help balance this, I have included more recipes from El Istmo than any other. The territory was the cradle of many of the prominent Mesoamerican civilizations and remains heavily influenced by the indigenous cultures that continue to thrive. Europeans gained a foothold here and settlement was not far behind. Many colonial-era buildings are still functioning as government offices, galleries, restaurants, shops, hotels, and private residences.

With such an abundant history and varied geography, it should be no surprise that the food is some of the richest and most exotic in the country while still clinging to its innocent, elegant simplicity. Many cooks take great pride in their adeptness with the cuisine of Spain, and that influence is evident in the diverse local and personal styles.

Oaxaca is widely known for its seven moles, but it has a good deal more to offer. From the Pacific costal region with fresh seafood and tropical fruits to the high-altitude cooking of the indigenous *Alto Mixtecas*, there is something for everyone. Insects and larvae are popular fare and the mezcal ranges from the almost gasoline-like, inexpensive renditions to the complex, smoky, aged-in-oak premium spirits. Long recognized in Mexico as a culinary seventh heaven, Oaxaca has been "discovered" by North American foodies and chefs in recent years. While the exotic is readily available, full-flavored, homey comfort foods abound for those with less courageous palates.

My experience in Tabasco is limited compared to the other two states. I have passed through on a number of journeys and have stayed overnight several times. The hot and steamy tropical lowlands are lush with fruits and vegetables, and cacao production is a major agricultural industry. During the colonial era, this region was somewhat isolated and consequently developed its own style. The food is influenced by the indigenous peoples, particularly the Maya, and has European roots as well. Many preparations as well as ingredients are unique to Tabasco, where even the names of ingredients available in other regions are known by their unique *Tabasqueña* monikers.

From the towering Mount Orizaba, the tallest in Mexico, to the lowland Cuenca of the Rio Papaloapan and the seemingly endless, nearly 600-mile-long Gulf Coast, Veracruz seems to have it all. The Totonaco culture, which invented and gave the calendar to the Mayans; Cortez, who first landed here at La Antigua on his journey to conquer the Aztecs; and the continuous trade with the Yucatán, the Caribbean, Africa, and Europe all have influenced the state.

A mixture of foods are featured in Veracruz. Tropical fruits and abundant seafood are consumed everywhere. Some of the European-influenced dishes are reinterpreted in each region (the high country, the plains, and the costal lowlands), resulting in at least three distinct versions of the same dish. The bustling Port of Veracruz boasts the music styles of traditional Jarana, Salsa, Afro-Caribbean, and Danzón, to name a few. The famous tomato-chile-olive sauce with almonds, *Salsa Veracruzana*, known throughout Mexico and the world is served in most restaurants. Coffee culture is everywhere, especially in the port—where *Café Parroquia* uses the largest espresso machine I have ever seen—and in the sophisticated capital and university city of Xalapa (Jalapa), situated in the foothills of the Sierra Madre less than an hour from the coffee plantations of Coatepec.

I cannot forget to mention vanilla. Native to Mexico and Central America, this exotic bean, actually a seed pod from a variety of orchid, is of major importance worldwide. In the town of Papantla, the aroma is ever-present, and the vanilla pods are used in both savory and sweet preparations and also as a material for local handicrafts.

I could write an entire book about the history, culture, and cooking of each state, but for now I will try to give you a little glimpse of the amazing food of this area.

Bocadillos
POTATO FRITTERS

SERVED THROUGHOUT OAXACA and in Mexico City, bocadillos are Oaxaca's answer to the latke. More commonly made with onions and eggs and served with hot salsa, this recipe, as served at the Oaxaca restaurant La Fonda de Santo Domingo is more of a dessert or sweet snack that uses cheese as a binder. Bocadillos make a great dessert, a snack with Café de Olla, Mexican Chocolate Caliente, or even as a breakfast or brunch item with eggs.

MAKES 6 TO 8 SERVINGS

1. Peel the potatoes while still warm, then mash them with the cheese, flour, and salt.

2. Shape the mixture into small, round, or oval patties about 1/2 inch thick.

3. Dredge in the flour, removing any excess.

4. Put enough vegetable oil or lard in a skillet to fill the pan about 1/2 inch deep. Fry at 360 degrees F on both sides until golden.

5. Drain well, dust with canela and powdered sugar, and serve immediately.

Note: Bocadillos are also great with maple syrup, fruit syrup, or honey instead of powdered sugar.

5 large potatoes, boiled with the skins on

8 ounces queso fresco, shredded*

2 tablespoons all-purpose flour

1/2 teaspoon salt

3/4 cup flour for dredging

Vegetable oil or lard for frying

2 teaspoons ground canela

1/2 cup powdered sugar

*Panela, ricotta, salada, or Monterey Jack cheese may be used

Robalo Relleno de Camarón y Jaiba
WHITEFISH STUFFED WITH SHRIMP AND CRAB

1 whole (6 to 8 pounds, gutted, and
  scaled) Róbalo (snook), sea bass,
  haddock, or snapper or 4 to 5
  pounds fish fillets of your choice

1/2 cup freshly squeezed lime juice

Salt and pepper to taste

1/2 cup olive oil

1 1/2 pounds small shrimp (bay
  shrimp work well here), peeled
  and deveined

1 small white onion, finely minced

1 pound lump crabmeat (I prefer
  blue crab)

1/4 cup chopped cilantro

4 bay leaves, toasted

25 leaves fresh oregano

2 red onions, sliced into 1/4-inch-
  thick rings

4 to 5 jalapeño chiles (poblano or
  Anaheim may be used for a
  milder effect), stemmed and sliced
  into rings 1/8 inch thick

6 cloves garlic, peeled and cut into
  fourths lengthwise

IN THE QUAINT LITTLE TOWN of Tlacotalpan, Veracruz, about 15 miles inland from the Gulf of Mexico, live my friends David McCauley and Rafael Aguilera. Rafa is an artist and his mother, Doña Rafaela, is a fantastic cook. My first encounter with her was a "light" lunch that she prepared for us at her home. It was a multi-course affair, culminating in a tour of her garden where she showed me the many herbs and vegetables that she used on a regular basis.

When I brought my first culinary group to visit Tlacotalpan, Doña Rafaela graciously agreed to give us a cooking demonstration. The menu consisted of a curried appetizer dip made from Tezmiche—a microscopic river creature that tasted like a mixture of crab and tuna—white rice, fresh handmade corn tortillas, and a stuffed local fish called Róbalo. It was one of the most delicious fish preparations I have ever enjoyed. The group was convinced that she had cooked enough to feed at least twice as many people as were present; however, there were almost no leftovers. Her recipe follows.

MAKES 8 TO 10 SERVINGS

1. Sprinkle a small amount of the lime juice inside and outside the entire fish, then season with salt and pepper.

2. Heat 3 tablespoons of the olive oil in a pan, season the shrimp with salt and pepper, and sauté with the minced onion until the shrimp is just pink. Remove from the heat and mix in the crab and cilantro.

3. Stuff the fish belly cavity with the shrimp and crab filling. (Note: If using fillets, you may butterfly a thick fillet to be stuffed or just place the filling in the foil first and top with the fish.)

4. Loosely line a baking sheet or roaster pan with aluminum foil and fold the edges upward to catch the juices.

5. Place the stuffed fish on the foil. Top with the bay leaves, oregano, onions, chiles, garlic, peppers, carrots, and tomatoes (in that order), all evenly distributed to cover the fish.

6. Sprinkle with the remaining lime juice, liberally salt and pepper, and drizzle with the rest of the olive oil.

7. Top with a toasted banana leaf (see page 29) or foil. Fold the edges of the bottom foil to create a sealed package.

8. Place in a 450-degree oven and bake for 25 to 30 minutes. Remove from the oven and allow to steam in the package for 10 more minutes.

9. Carefully open the package, avoiding the hot steam. Place the fish on a serving platter and spoon the juices that have collected over the top.

2 sweet red or yellow bell peppers, stemmed and sliced into rings 1/4 inch thick

2 medium carrots, peeled and sliced thin or julienned

6 to 8 roma or plum tomatoes, sliced into 1/4-inch rounds

Banana leaves or foil to wrap the fish

Manchamanteles
FRUITY RED MOLE

10 ancho chiles

6 to 8 guajillos or costeños chiles

2 to 3 pasillas Oaxaqueñas or
   chipotles secos

1 large white onion, roughly
   chopped

1/4 cup almond slices, toasted

1/3 cup peanuts, roasted or
   1/4 cup creamy peanut butter

4 whole allspice

1/2 teaspoon black peppercorns

1/4 cup raisins, soaked in warm
   water

1 tablespoon dried Mexican
   oregano, toasted

8 cloves garlic, toasted with the
   skin on and then peeled

1 1/2 quarts Caldo de Pollo
   (see page 138) or water

1/3 cup (approximate) vegetable
   oil or lard

5 or 6 medium ripe roma tomatoes,
   well charred, pureed, and
   strained

MANCHAMANTELES, ONE OF THE SEVEN MOLES OF OAXACA, translates as "tablecloth stainer." This intensely colored, hot, fruity-sweet concoction certainly can wreak havoc with your table linens, not to mention your kitchen; however, it is well worth the potential mess.

I developed this recipe from several that I have encountered in Oaxaca, Mexico City, and Xalapa, Veracruz (as you might guess from the addition of chipotle chiles). Although it is traditionally served with pieces of chicken cooked in the mole along with pork neck bones, *manchamanteles* is a very versatile sauce. You can bake whole pork loin or chicken in a covered casserole with the sauce or mix a cup of it with 1/8 cup of vinegar and use as a marinade for chicken breasts, pork chops, or tenderloin to be char-grilled (serve more sauce with the meat after it is cooked). Since it is a complicated and somewhat messy recipe, I usually prepare double quantities so that I can freeze half for later use.

MAKES 8 TO 10 SERVINGS

1. Toast the chiles on a griddle or heavy skillet, stem, seed, and soak for 15 to 20 minutes (see page 21). Puree and strain.

2. In a heavy skillet, fry the onion until it begins to color; add the nuts, allspice, and peppercorns and fry for 2 to 3 minutes more. Remove from heat and add the raisins, oregano, and garlic. Puree with 2 cups of the caldo or water until smooth.

3. In a Dutch oven (you may use a skillet, but the tall sides of the Dutch oven help to minimize the mess), fry the chile puree in 3 tablespoons of the oil or lard. Cook for 10 to 12 minutes, stirring often, until the mixture thickens. Add the strained tomatoes, canela, and cloves and cook for 10 to 15 minutes more.

4. Add the nut-and-spice puree and the ground sesame seeds and cook for 10 more minutes. Add the rest of the caldo, piloncillo or brown sugar, and vinegar and reduce heat to simmer.

5. In a skillet, fry the plantains in 2 tablespoons oil or lard for 2 to 3 minutes, and then add the pineapple chunks. Fry for 3 to 4 minutes more, and then add to the mole with the salt. Remove the canela, puree again, and simmer for 15 to 20 minutes more, adding more water if the mixture gets too thick.

1 to 1 1/2 inches of canela

4 whole cloves

1/3 cup sesame seeds, toasted and ground in a spice grinder

1 tablespoon piloncillo or brown sugar

2 tablespoons vinegar (pineapple or cider)

2 ripe plantains, peeled and sliced

1 1/2 cups fresh pineapple, cut into 1/2-inch dice

2 teaspoons salt

Huachinango Veracruzano
VERACRUZ-STYLE RED SNAPPER

THE VERACRUZ STYLE is firmly rooted in the Mediterranean with French, African, and Caribbean influences. *Huachinango* means red snapper, although around the lively fish markets in the vibrant Port of Veracruz many different types of fish are offered with this exotic sauce made from fresh tomatoes, olives, capers, and almonds, spiked with the jalapeño , which is almost the state fruit. Variations abound, and I have used poblano chiles in place of the sweet peppers that many cooks prefer.

MAKES 8 TO 10 SERVINGS

1. Score the skin side of the fish 1/4 inch deep and 1 1/2 inches apart with a sharp knife. Place in a nonreactive dish and sprinkle with the lime juice. Marinate 10 to 15 minutes.

2. Heat a little of the olive oil in a skillet and toast the bread slices until golden brown on both sides. Cool and then process to fine crumbs.

3. Preheat a large, deep sauté or roasting pan. Season both sides of the fish with salt and pepper, sear in the olive oil skin-side first until color begins to develop. Remove the fish to a plate or pan.

4. In the same pan, sauté the onions, then the garlic; add the chiles, tomatoes, raisins if using, and capers and cook for 3 to 4 minutes, stirring frequently. Add the olives, almonds, bay leaves, chives, canela, half of the cilantro, sherry vinegar, breadcrumbs, and enough water, broth, or tomato juice to make a medium-thick sauce. Place the fish in the sauce, cover, and reduce to simmer. Cook 6 to 8 minutes for fillets and 10 to 12 minutes for whole fish. Uncover, gently stir, raise heat to medium-high, and cook 2 more minutes. Garnish with remaining cilantro and serve immediately.

3 1/2- to 4-pound red snapper whole fish or fish fillets, scaled and cleaned

Juice of 1 lime

1/3 to 1/2 cup olive oil

2 slices French bread

Salt and pepper to taste

1 large white onion, diced

2 to 3 cloves garlic, chopped

2 fresh poblano chiles, roasted, peeled, and diced

4 whole pickled chiles (jalapeño , serrano, or mild yellow), minced

6 to 8 medium roma tomatoes, diced

1/2 cup raisins (optional)

2 to 3 tablespoons capers

1/2 cup chopped green olives

1/2 cup sliced toasted almonds

3 bay leaves, toasted

2 tablespoons chopped chives or scallion tops

1 or 2 sticks of canela (optional)

1/2 bunch cilantro, coarsely chopped

1/8 cup sherry vinegar

1/4 to 3/4 cup water as needed

Tamales de Anís
SWEET ANISE-SEED TAMALES

I FIRST TASTED THESE TAMALES on the day I met Doña Angela in Xalapa, Veracruz. We had them for breakfast with some savory tamales and peanut-chipotle salsa. This recipe comes from Doña Carmen Alegre, one of the most impressive tamale cooks I know. She and her husband Juan make 4 or 5 varieties that they sell next to the church on Sunday evenings in Tlacotalpan.

These tamales are simple, yet rich and sweet. You could add or substitute cloves and canela for the anise seeds and also add nuts if you like. They work great as a breakfast item or as a dessert.

MAKES 24 TAMALES

1 cup butter or vegetable shortening

1 1/2 pounds prepared masa for tamales

2 tablespoons anise seeds, lightly toasted

2 teaspoons salt

1/4 cup sugar

1/2 cup raisins or prunes, chopped

2 dozen cornhusks, soaked

1. Whip the butter or vegetable shortening at high speed until fluffy.

2. Slowly add the masa in small increments. When all of the masa is incorporated, whip on high for about 2 minutes.

3. Reduce the speed and add the anise seed, salt, sugar, and raisins or prunes.

4. Spread about 2 tablespoons of masa on the center of each cornhusk.

5. Wrap in a tamale shape and steam for 1 hour and 15 minutes.

6. Cool for 10 to 15 minutes before serving. The tamales may be reheated in the steamer or briefly in the microwave.

Tapiste
VERACRUZ-STYLE CHICKEN STEAMED IN BANANA LEAVES WITH GREEN HERB SAUCE

2 fryer-sized chickens (2 1/2 to 3
1/2 pounds) or 1 roaster-sized
chicken (4 1/2 to 7 pound), cut
into serving-sized pieces

1 large white onion, peeled and
sliced in 1/2-inch-thick rounds

12 to 15 cloves of garlic, peeled
(no elephant garlic)

5 or 6 jalapeño chiles, stems
removed and split in half lengthwise

8 to 12 tomatillos, husked
(see page 27)

4 to 5 ounces (about 36) fresh
acuyo or Hoja Santa leaves

1 to 1 1/2 cups cool water or
chicken broth

Juice of 2 limes

2 tablespoons salt

3 tablespoons olive or vegetable oil

1/2 pounds of fresh or frozen
banana leaves

I LEARNED THIS RECIPE in the kitchen of Doña Angela in Xalapa (Jalapa), the capital of Veracruz. Doña Angela's small (5 table) restaurant serves truly home-style, comida corrida to a loyal following of neighborhood customers Monday through Saturday. I was strolling past with my friend, Roy Dudley, on a Sunday morning and was invited in to join her, her daughter, and grand-daughter for a tamale breakfast. She was gracious enough to allow me to assist her the next day with the preparation of Monday's menu, Tapiste. A very special and memorable personal experience to be sure. A hands-on class with Doña Angela is now part of my group culinary tours to Veracruz.

Tapiste is a traditional dish of southern Veracruz and can be prepared with chicken or fish. The leaf of the Acuyo, also called Hoja Santa (Piper Auritum), with its anise-like, peppery quality, is the key flavor in this dish; however, I have created a substitute and, although not exactly the same, the results are tasty and worth the effort.

MAKES 8 TO 10 SERVINGS

3 firm, but not too green, plantains or 5 medium, waxy potatoes, peeled and sliced into 3/8-inch-thick rounds

FOR THE TAPISTE

1. Roast the onions, garlic, chiles, and tomatillos on a comal or heavy skillet until well browned and somewhat blackened (see techniques chapter).

2. Place the roasted ingredients and the acuyo into a blender with half of the water or chicken broth. Blend thoroughly, adding more liquid as needed, until a smooth green puree is formed.

3. Place the puree in a nonreactive bowl or pan and add the lime juice, salt, and oil. Mix well and take 1 cup out to reserve for the plantains.

4. Place the chicken in the bowl with the "mole" and marinate for 30 minutes.

5. Meanwhile, place the sliced plantains or potatoes in another container with the reserved puree and marinate alongside the chicken.

6. Toast the banana leaves to prepare them for wrapping (see page 29). Cut them into sheets large enough to wrap around each piece of meat 3 to 4 times (about 18 x 18 inches).

7. Place each piece of chicken and several plantain or potato slices on a banana leaf and fold to create a square or rectangular sealed package and tie with a strip of the leaf.

8. Arrange in a steamer or tamale pot, taking care to leave room for the steam to circulate. Cover the Tapiste with a layer of banana leaves to trap the steam and cover with the lid. Heat the water in the steamer to boiling then reduce heat to a slow steady boil.

9. Cook for 1 1/4 to 1 1/2 hours, adding water as needed to prevent the steamer from going dry.

10. Turn off the steamer, remove the lid and allow the packets to cool for at least 10 minutes before removing the Tapiste from the pot. May be served individually in the packets or removed and arranged on a platter.

FOR THE ACUYO SUBSTITUTE

The following substitute may be used for acuyo when none is available.

1/2 pound fresh green fennel tops

6 sprigs flat-leafed parsley

1/2 teaspoon anise seed

1 teaspoon whole black pepper

1/2 teaspoon whole coriander seed

1 teaspoon whole allspice

3 dried avocado leaves or
  2 tablespoons fresh or dried tarragon

1. Mix the fennel tops and parsley together; set aside. Toast anise seed, pepper, coriander seed, and allspice; grind together. Mix in with fennel tops and add avocado leaves or tarragon.

Cóctel de Camarón con Chipotle y Aguacate

SHRIMP COCKTAIL WITH AVOCADO
AND CHIPOTLE CHILES

FOR THE SHRIMP

2 teaspoons whole allspice

1 teaspoon whole black peppercorns

1 teaspoon coriander seeds

3 to 4 bay leaves

3 quarts water

1 tablespoon salt

Juice of 1 lime

1 1/2 pounds shrimp, peeled and
   deveined

FOR THE COCKTAIL

1 cup peeled, seeded, and diced
   cucumber

1/2 cup diced red onion, rinsed
   (see page 19)

2 to 3 tablespoons finely chopped
   chipotle chiles en adobo plus
   1 tablespoon of the juice from
   the chiles

1/2 cup ketchup

1 tablespoon olive oil

1/2 bunch cilantro, finely chopped

3 ripe avocados, diced

Salt and lime juice to taste

I HAVE ALWAYS BEEN INTRIGUED by the Mexican shrimp cocktail. On my first trip beyond the border, I tasted a fresh Mexican shrimp cocktail and returned home to try to duplicate it. My efforts were tasty, yet I was unable to capture the flavor I was seeking. Finally I listened to my Mexican friends and tried ketchup in the recipe. That was it! My friend Noe Cano, from Veracruz, helped me develop this version using chipotle instead of the classic fresh jalapeño . You can try it both ways.

MAKES 8 TO 10 SERVINGS

1. Toast the allspice, peppercorns, coriander, and bay leaves to release the flavors and place all in a cheesecloth sachet to make later removal easier.

2. Bring 3 quarts of water to a boil; add the salt and the sachet of spices. Boil for 8 to 10 minutes.

3. On high heat, add the lime juice and the shrimp and bring back to a boil. Remove from heat and let sit 1 minute.

4. Drain immediately, reserving and cooling 3/4 cup of the cooking liquid. Discard the sachet.

5. Spread the shrimp out on a tray or large pan and refrigerate until cool.

6. Mix all of the ingredients (including the reserved cooking liquid) except the avocado, salt, and lime juice, and chill for 30 minutes to 2 hours.

7. Mix in the avocado and season with salt and lime juice. Serve immediately.

Pollo en Escabeche Oriental
EASTERN-STYLE SOUSED CHICKEN

FOR THE CHICKEN

1/3 cup vegetable oil

8 bone-in chicken quarters

Salt and pepper to taste

FOR THE SOUSE

1 large white onion, peeled and cut into 1/4-inch strips

4 cloves garlic, peeled

1 medium carrot, peeled and julienned

2 serrano or jalapeño chiles, split in half lengthwise

2 or 3 toasted chiles de árbol, chiltepin, or japonés

6 allspice berries, toasted and cracked

1/2 teaspoon whole coriander, toasted

8 whole cloves

6 whole peppercorns

4 bay leaves, toasted

1 sprig each of fresh thyme and marjoram

ESCABECHE IS A TERM FROM SPANISH COOKING that means "marinated" or "pickled." This recipe is a little of both. I enjoyed this rendition during an unannounced meal stop at a little roadside café on highway 190 while traveling on the bus between Oaxaca and the Port of Salinas Cruz on the way to Huatulco on the Pacific coastline. You may serve Pollo en Escabeche Oriental the same day it is made but the flavor will improve with a day or two of refrigeration. The charcoal-grilling option is something I learned in the Yucatan. The smokiness goes well with the sweet and sour aromatic flavors. The leftovers are excellent for tacos, tostadas, and quesadillas, or in chicken salad.

MAKES 8 SERVINGS

1. Place all of the souse ingredients except the lime or orange juice in a nonreactive saucepan and heat to boiling. Reduce heat and simmer for 15 minutes.

2. Preheat a large skillet or Dutch oven and add the oil. Salt and pepper the chicken, and then brown the seasoned chicken pieces on all sides.

3. Place the chicken in a casserole or roasting pan small enough that the chicken can be closely packed.

4. Pour the warm souse over the chicken and cover with a tight-fitting lid or foil.

5. Place in a 350-degree-F oven and bake for 35 minutes, then remove from the oven.

1 cup mild vinegar (pineapple,
apple cider, or rice are best)

2 1/4 cups water

1/4 cup piloncillo or brown sugar

1 teaspoon salt

Juice of 1 lime or orange to finish
after cooking

6. Carefully open the cover and turn over the chicken pieces, add the lime or orange juice, re-cover the pan, and let cool. Refrigerate. Remove the chicken from the souse after at least 4 but no more than 12 hours. Reserve the vegetables for garnish.

7. Reheat in the oven or over a charcoal grill.

Manilla

VERACRUZ-STYLE MINCED FISH

I first tasted this dish in Tlacotalpan, Veracruz, and then had it again a few days later in Monte Pio, a small, sleepy, Gulf Coast village. It is a truly hair-raising two-hour ride in the back of a small pickup from Catemaco, the lakeside city famous for its witches. In Veracruz this dish is usually prepared with a type of perch. Any fresh fish, lump crabmeat, or good quality canned tuna packed in water will work. A dish similar to manilla is made in Mazatlan, Sinaloa, where smoked marlin is used. Manilla serves as a delicious filling for empanadas, tacos, chile rellenos, or tortas, or as a salad or main dish.

MAKES ABOUT 4 1/4 CUPS

1. If using fresh fish, heat the salted caldo to boiling, add the fish fillet, reduce heat, and simmer for about 10 minutes until fish is flaky.

2. Remove the fish from the caldo and cool. With a fork, finely shred the fish.

3. Combine the fish or tuna with the remaining ingredients, except the olive or vegetable oil, and mix well.

4. Taste to adjust the seasonings. Mix in the oil.

5. Let sit for 15 to 20 minutes to develop the flavor, then serve or refrigerate until ready to use.

1 quart Caldo de Pescado (see page 141) with 2 teaspoons salt

2 1/2 pounds fish fillets or 3 15-ounce cans solid, water-packed tuna

1 medium white onion, finely chopped

3 cloves garlic, minced

6 plum tomatoes, diced

1 fresh or pickled jalapeño *

1/3 cup chopped, pimento-stuffed green olives

1 tablespoon coarsely chopped capers

1 teaspoon toasted Mexican oregano

Juice of 1 lime

1 teaspoon vinegar (pineapple, apple cider, or rice)

1/4 cup chopped parsley or cilantro

Salt and pepper

1/3 to 1/2 cup olive oil or vegetable oil

*A finely minced serrano chile or chipotle en adobe may be substituted.

Chilpachole de Jaiba
CRAB AND EPAZOTE STEW
WITH CHIPOTLE AND TOMATO

2 1/2 quarts water

1 teaspoon salt

2 bay leaves, lightly toasted

1 medium white onion

3 cloves raw garlic, peeled

4 cloves garlic, roasted and peeled
(see page 23)

1 teaspoon whole black
peppercorns

4 whole allspice berries or 4 whole
cloves (optional)

8 to 10 small live crabs, scrubbed
and rinsed (or cooked whole
Dungeness crabs, blue crabs, or
crab legs, about 2 1/2 to 3
pounds total)

4 or 5 small ripe tomatoes, roasted
until almost completely black
(see page 27)

1 to 2 ancho chiles, toasted,
stemmed, seeded then soaked to
rehydrate (see page 25)

THIS SEDUCTIVE COMBINATION of flavors in Chilpachole de Jaiba is popular along the Gulf Coast from Veracruz to Tampico. I first tasted it during my stint as sous chef for Mark Miller at the Coyote Café in Santa Fe. In Veracruz, the small blue crabs are purchased alive and then cooked whole, but you can make a tasty version using precooked whole crab or crab legs. Prawns or shrimp can be used alone or in combination with the crab. Often served as a soup course, this flavorful stew makes a great lunch or supper main course along with Empanadas de Queso and rice.

MAKES 4 TO 6 SERVINGS AS MAIN COURSE

1. Bring water to boil in a soup pot or kettle. Add the salt, bay leaves, half of the onion, the raw garlic, peppercorns, and allspice. Boil 6 to 8 minutes.

2. Place the crabs in the pot and return to a boil. Reduce the heat to medium and continue cooking for about 6 minutes until the crabs turn bright reddish orange. Remove the crabs to cool.

Note: If using precooked crab, cook the water with the seasonings only—not the crab—and proceed to the next step.

3. Break open the crabs to remove the meat, discarding the gill-like membrane. If you find any of the orange-colored roe, scrape it into a separate bowl to enrich the broth later. (For a more impressive presentation, when using small whole crabs, you may want to save one whole crab or the claws of one crab per bowl, and only open the top shell to allow for removal of the gill membrane.)

4. Place the picked-over shells in the broth and simmer covered for 30 to 40 minutes. Strain.

5. Puree the tomatoes, roasted garlic, rehydrated ancho chiles, and remaining onion in a blender or food processor until smooth. Heat the oil in a heavy pan or skillet until hot enough to just begin smoking. Carefully add the tomato puree and fry, stirring constantly for about 3 minutes. Add the strained broth, chipotle chiles, and epazote and simmer covered for 20 to 30 minutes.

6. Remove the epazote and skim off any excess fat. Remove from the heat, add the crabmeat, any roe, and whole crabs or claws, if any, cover and let sit for about 5 minutes to reheat the crab. Serve in bowls with lime wedges.

2 to 3 chipotle chiles en adobo, chopped

2 tablespoons vegetable oil

2 to 3 sprigs fresh epazote or 1 teaspoon toasted Mexican oregano

Limes to garnish

VARIATIONS

You could substitute whole prawns (with heads, if you can find them) for the crab and use fish broth or chicken stock instead of water. Cook with the shell on for flavor and peel if desired before serving. In Puebla, a version of Chilpachole is prepared using a whole chicken in place of the crab.

Pescado Ajillo
FISH FILLET WITH CHILES AND GARLIC

AFTER TRYING THIS DISH on a family vacation to Huatulco, Oaxaca, my youngest son, Tristan, the picky eater, became a fish enthusiast. Cooked using a portable gas burner, this recipe was served at a beachside palapa restaurant in Bahía Maguey, one of the picturesque bays. The results were stunning.

MAKES 6 TO 8 SERVINGS

1. Place the oil in a preheated skillet. Cut the stemmed and seeded chiles into 1/8 x 1 1/2-inch strips with scissors or a sharp knife. Add the chile strips and garlic to the skillet. Stir constantly until the garlic is golden brown.

2. Strain the chiles and garlic and reserve, then return the oil to the pan.

3. Season the fish with salt and pepper. Sauté over medium-high heat until both sides are nicely browned.

4. Remove the fish and add the lime juice and caldo or water and the chiles and garlic. Cook for 1 minute.

5. Place the fish on a serving platter and pour the sauce, chiles, and garlic over the top. Serve immediately.

1/3 cup olive or vegetable oil

4 ancho chiles (guajillo if you want it hotter), stemmed and seeded

8 to 10 cloves garlic, peeled and sliced thin, lengthwise

3 to 3 1/2 pounds fish fillet (mahimahi, sea bass, snook, snapper, and so on)

Salt and pepper

1/4 cup lime juice

2/3 cup Caldo de Pescado (see page 141) or water

Helado de Coco
COCONUT ICE CREAM

THIS ICE CREAM, popular in Tlacotalpan, Veracruz, became a favorite of mine during several visits. Made from fresh coconuts, it is offered on the street corners by vendors who make it in their homes. I developed this recipe to satisfy my cravings for this refreshing treat.

MAKES JUST OVER 1 GALLON

1. Blend the arrowroot powder with 1/4 cup of the milk until smooth.

2. Combine this with the rest of the milk, half-and-half, and coconut milk; place in a cooking pot along with the vanilla bean and sugar.

   Note: If using vanilla extract, do not add until the cooking process is complete.

3. Warm over medium heat until almost boiling, stirring constantly.

4. Carefully combine 1 cup of the hot mixture with the eggs to temper.

5. Mix the tempered eggs and the rest of the milk together and bring to a gentle boil. Reduce heat and simmer for 5 minutes while stirring constantly.

6. Cool completely, discard the vanilla bean, and place in an ice cream freezer. Follow your freezer's directions.

2 teaspoons arrowroot powder or cornstarch

1/2 gallon whole milk

1 quart half-and-half

4 cans unsweetened coconut milk

1 vanilla bean, cut in half lengthwise, or 2 tablespoons premium vanilla extract

1 1/2 cups sugar*

1 whole egg plus 3 egg yolks, well beaten

1/2 teaspoon salt

*Raw or turbinado sugar tastes more like the sugar used in Mexico

Salsa de Cacahuate
PEANUT AND CHIPOTLE-CHILE SALSA

1 cup raw peanuts

1 tablespoon vegetable or
    peanut oil

1/2 medium onion, dry roasted

3 cloves garlic, peeled and roasted

1 to 2 chipotle chiles en adobo

3 medium tomatoes, well roasted

1 tablespoon vinegar (pineapple or
    apple cider)

2 tablespoons cold water

1/8 cup chopped cilantro

Salt to taste

THIS SALSA IS ANOTHER EXAMPLE OF GLOBAL INFLUENCES on Mexican cooking. The smoky chipotle chile from Veracruz blends remarkably well with the peanut that originated in Africa. I learned this salsa from Doña Angela in Xalapa. She served it with Tamales de Anís (see page 85). It also works well as a dip with grilled pork or with many tacos.

MAKES 2 CUPS

1. Fry the peanuts in the oil until golden brown (about 3 minutes).

2. Grind all ingredients except the cilantro and salt in a molcajete or blender until somewhat smooth, yet still grainy.

3. Stir in the cilantro and salt to taste.

Arroz Verde
GREEN RICE

THIS RECIPE MAKES STRIKING LOOKING RICE with great flavor. Arroz Verde goes well with most Mexican plates, especially seafood. At home, we cook the leftovers with scrambled eggs. You will find many other uses for it as well.

MAKES 6 TO 8 SERVINGS

1. Puree the spinach or dark lettuce leaves, chiles, cilantro, and green onion tops in a blender with half of the water.

2. Heat the oil in a saucepan. Add the rice and sauté, stirring constantly, until the grains turn white with a little browning.

3. Add the salt, spinach puree, and the remaining water.

4. Bring the liquid to a boil; stir well, and then cover tightly. Reduce heat to very low and cook for 15 minutes.

5. Remove from heat (keep covered—no peeking!) and steam for 10 minutes more.

6. Fluff with a spoon or fork and serve.

1/2 pound spinach or dark lettuce leaves

1 poblano or 2 jalapeño chiles, roasted, peeled, and seeded

1 bunch cilantro

2 green onion tops, chopped

2 cups water

3 tablespoons vegetable oil

1 1/2 cups long grain rice

2 teaspoons salt

Pierna de Cerdo Adobada
CHILE-SPICED ROAST PORK LEG

PIERNA DE CERDO ADOBADA is a typical preparation with variations found throughout Mexico, the American Southwest, Latin
America, and even the Philippines. The uses for pork en adobo
are endless—from a main course for a formal meal to taco fillings, tamales, tortas, and various antojitos.

MAKES 8 TO 10 SERVINGS

1. Toast the allspice berries, coriander seeds, and cumin seeds (see
   page 25). Make the chile-soaking liquid by combining all ingredients for liquid (see next page). Toast, seed, and soak the chiles in
   the liquid.

2. Blend oregano and epazote with the spices and chiles, adding about
   1/3 cup or more of the chile-soaking liquid to make a paste about
   the same thickness as tomato paste.

   *Note: This is one case where the blender has a definite advantage
   over the molecajete or metate. The latter two do work; however,
   the effort is almost as great as the mess you may create.*

3. Carefully pierce the surface of the pork leg (both the fat side and
   the meaty side) with a paring knife or the tip of a sharp chef's knife
   about 2 inches deep or to the bone. Reinsert the knife in the same
   place at a 90-degree angle to the first cut to create a cross-shaped
   incision. Repeat this at random intervals of about 3 to 4 inches
   apart; about 20 or so total cross-shaped cuts will suffice.

4. Rub the chile paste over the surface of the pork leg, pressing some
   into each incision.

5. Seal in a plastic bag or in a nonreactive pan and cover. Refrigerate
   at least 6 hours or overnight.

FOR THE PORK

6 medium-sized ancho chiles

3 guajillo or New Mexico red chiles

*2 to 3 cascabel chiles (or
   1 additional guajillo)*

*1 or 2 chipotle or mora chiles
   (either dried or en adobo)*

1 tablespoon whole allspice berries

1 teaspoon whole coriander seeds

*1/2 teaspoon whole cumin seeds
   (optional)*

1 to 2 tablespoons Mexican oregano

*1 sprig fresh epazote or 2 table-
   spoons dried epazote **

*Pork arm roast (6 to 10 pounds,
   bone-in) or Boston butt*

**If you have no epazote, you
   may substitute fresh thyme,
   marjoram, or bay leaf, or any
   combination of the three. The
   taste will be slightly different,
   but still flavorful and good.*

FOR CHILI-SOAKING LIQUID

1/4 cup cider vinegar

2 tablespoons honey or brown sugar

1 medium white onion

8 to 12 cloves garlic

1 1/2 teaspoon salt

6. Place in a covered electric countertop roaster, or in the oven in a loosely covered roasting pan and bake at 350 degrees for 4 1/2 to 6 hours depending on the size of your pork leg. Baste with the cooking juices every 30 to 45 minutes. The meat should be fork-tender and still juicy with some crispy edges.

7. Allow the meat to rest for 20 to 30 minutes before you cut or shred the pork. This will allow the juices to reabsorb into the meat, making it more flavorful and juicy.

8. You can make a sauce from the pan drippings if you cool them and then skim off the excess fat (there will be quite a bit). This fat is also great for homemade lard. The remaining sauce will be rich from the meat and hot from the chiles. I usually strain it to remove any large pieces of chiles and spices.

Pay de Queso con Piña
CHEESE PIE WITH PINEAPPLES

I DEVELOPED THIS PIE RECIPE along with Noe Cano, my good friend, and the sous chef at the Santa Fe School of Cooking, where I teach. Noe is originally from Chacaltianguis, Veracruz, along the Rio Papaloapan, about forty-five minutes upriver from Tlacotalpan. The traditional version of this recipe uses requesón (ricotta cheese), but cream cheese works equally well. Visitors to Mexico are often surprised to see the many types of *pay* (pie). It is a very popular dessert. A traditional piecrust may replace the cookie crust called for in the recipe. This recipe may also be prepared substituting other fruits (apples, peaches, and so on) or simply made without the fruit.

1. Mix together crust ingredients except for the egg white, and press into a 9-inch pie or spring-form pan or a 9 x 13–inch glass baking dish, forming a lip 1 inch high around the edges. Carefully brush the inside of the crust with the egg white. Bake at 350 degrees F for 6 minutes. Remove from oven and cool.

2. For the filling, cream the ricotta or cream cheese and 1/4 cup of the sugar in a mixer until smooth. Continue mixing and add the whole eggs and yolks one at a time. Whip on high speed until fluffy (about 3 to 4 minutes). With mixer on low, slowly add the milks, vanilla, and lime juice.

3. Pour into prebaked crust. Gently place pineapple chunks on top to cover the surface evenly. Sprinkle with remaining 1/8 cup sugar and a dash of salt.

4. Bake at 350 degrees F for 35 to 40 minutes until filling is set (but not too firm) and top surface is light golden brown. Cool and serve.

FOR THE CRUST

1 3/4 cup shortbread-cookie or vanilla-wafer crumbs

1/4 cup butter, melted

1/8 cup sugar

1 1/2 teaspoon ground canela

1/4 teaspoon salt

1 egg white, lightly beaten until smooth

FOR THE FILLING

12 ounces soft ricotta or cream cheese, room temperature

1/4 cup + 1/8 cup sugar (raw or turbindo is best)

3 whole eggs

2 egg yolks

1 13-ounce can sweetened condensed milk

1 4-ounce can evaporated milk

1 tablespoon Mexican vanilla extract

3 tablespoons lime juice

1 cup diced or sliced pineapple

Dash of salt

Cecina Enchilada
CHILE-MARINATED PORK IN THIN SHEETS

1 teaspoon whole black peppercorns

3 whole cloves

1 teaspoon whole allspice

1 teaspoon Oaxaca or Mexican
oregano

1 2-inch piece of canela

4 to 5 chiles guajillos, toasted,
stemmed, seeded, and soaked

2 to 3 chiles anchos, toasted,
stemmed, seeded, and soaked

1/2 cup water or chile-soaking
liquid

2/3 cup vinegar (pineapple, apple
cider, or rice)

10 cloves garlic, peeled

2 teaspoons salt

1 tablespoon piloncillo or
brown sugar

1 tablespoons ounce ground
achiote or achiote paste (optional)

2 pounds boneless pork loin butter-
flied into thin sheets no more
than 1/4 inch thick*

*You can also use a boneless center-
cut loin or sirloin chops pounded
thin between two sheets of plastic.

CECINA ENCHILADA IS A MARKET SPECIALTY IN OAXACA; visitors
often see the sheets of pork, covered with the brick-red chile
paste, hanging like laundry in the carnecería (butcher) stalls. This
sight can be a little daunting for most Norteamericanos; however,
you can prepare a delicious rendition of Cecina Enchilada and
still follow all of the safe-food rules.

Cecina Enchilada is often prepared using beef instead of pork
and is called *tásajo;* I use sirloin, round, or chuck steak. The term
enchilada can be a little confusing, but it merely refers to being
covered in chile. The rolled corn tortilla concoction most of us
associate with that name north of the border is also an enchilada
because it is covered in chile, too. Cecina can be used as a filling
for tortilla enchiladas and tacos or as a main dish accompanied
by grilled onions, Chile Poblano Rajas or Chiles Jalapeños en
Escabeche (see pages 206, 51), guacamole, lime, cilantro, and
fresh tortillas.

MAKES 6 TO 8 SERVINGS

1. Toast the spices except canela in a skillet.

2. Blend all the spices with the chiles, vinegar, garlic, salt, piloncillo or
brown sugar, achiote if using, and 1/4 to 1/2 cup of the chile-soaking liquid or water until smooth.

3. Rub the sheets of pork meat with the paste and refrigerate, loosely
covered to promote drying, for at least 2 hours or up to one day.

4. About 20 to 30 minutes prior to cooking, take the pork out of the
refrigerator and uncover. (This will help to dry it, and it will cook
more evenly when warmed slightly before cooking.)

5. Cook over wood, charcoal, gas flame, or on a comal or griddle.

Pasta de Chile Seco Xiqueño
VERACRUZ-STYLE CHIPOTLE-CHILE SEASONING PASTE

Vegetable oil

25 to 30 chipotle seco chiles, stemmed

1/4 cup piloncillo or dark brown sugar, dissolved in 1 3/4 cups boiling water

8 to 12 cloves garlic, peeled

1/4 teaspoon ground cloves

1/2 teaspoon ground canela

1 teaspoon salt

THE FLAVOR OF THIS SEASONING PASTE is an essential component of the cooking of the state of Veracruz. It is smoky, hot, and slightly sweet with much complexity. I have emulated the Suarez de Galvan family's style from their small factory just outside of Xico in the coffee-growing foothills of Cofre de Perrote, an almost 14,000-foot volcanic peak in western Veracruz.

Chipotle chiles are smoked and dried jalapeño chiles used throughout Mexico. The dark red (almost black) and slightly sweet mora or moritas varieties are best. Jalapeño chiles, originally called *chiles curásemos*, reportedly derive their name from Jalapa (Xalapa), Veracruz. Apparently, an entrepreneur from Xalapa began packing pickled chiles at his factory in the city sometime in the 1930s or '40s and distributed them all around Mexico. The cans were labeled "Chiles de Jalapa" and eventually the chiles became universally known as jalapeños.

The paste will keep for several months in the refrigerator and up to a year in the freezer. It is useful for marinades, to enrich and enliven other sauces, or as a table condiment when thinned with a little water.

MAKES ABOUT 1 CUP

1. Heat a heavy skillet or saucepan with 1/4 inch or so of vegetable oil until hot (about 350 degrees F).

2. Place the chiles, 1/3 to 1/2 at a time, depending on the size of your pan, and fry until well toasted, aromatic, and deep brown in color (2 to 3 minutes). Strain the chiles and place them in the hot sugar-water to soak. Continue until all have been cooked.

3. Cook the garlic cloves in the same oil until well browned but not burnt.

4. Place the chiles, sugar water, garlic, cloves, canela, and salt in a blender and puree until smooth.

5. Pour off the excess oil and heat the skillet again.

6. Fry the puree, stirring well, for 2 to 3 minutes, then reduce the heat and simmer for 15 to 20 minutes until fairly thick.

7. Store in a glass jar or freezer bag.

Camarones Enchipotlados
SHRIMP IN HOT AND SMOKY CHIPOTLE SAUCE

CAMARONES ENCHIPOTLADOS is one of my favorite dishes! We used a buttery version of this to top small corn griddlecakes for an appetizer at the Coyote Café. I have since refined it a number of times and, after repeatedly eating it and watching it prepared in the state of Veracruz, where it is a tradition, I think I may have it almost perfected. You can make a tasty version of it with chipotle chiles en adobo, but the deep, spicy, complex flavor of the Veracruzano Pasta de Chile Seco goes way beyond tasty to soul satisfying. These shrimp are suitable as a main dish, appetizer, or in tacos, served either hot or cold.

MAKES 6 TO 8 SERVINGS

1. Blend the garlic with the tomatoes and onion, adding a little water if needed to facilitate the blending.

2. Season the shrimp with salt and pepper.

3. Heat a large sauté pan or Dutch oven and add the oil.

4. Sauté the shrimp on very high heat until half cooked and beginning to brown. Remove the shrimp from the pan with a slotted spoon.

5. Fry the sauce in the oil for about 2 minutes along with the Pasta de Chile Seco or the chipotle chiles en adobo, stirring frequently to prevent burning.

6. Add the shrimp, stir well to coat, and cook the shrimp through. The sauce should be fairly thick, adhering to the shrimp.

7. Add the lime juice and the cilantro, stir again, and serve hot or chilled.

6 to 8 cloves garlic, peeled and roasted

3 ripe tomatoes, well roasted, or charred (see page 27)

1 medium white onion, thickly sliced and pan roasted until well caramelized (see page 23)

2 1/2 pounds shrimp, deveined (and peeled, if desired)

Salt to taste

Freshly ground black pepper to taste

1/4 cup olive oil

2 to 3 chipotle chiles en adobo, finely chopped, along with a pinch of ground cloves and 1/2 teaspoon ground canela

Juice of 2 limes or 1 orange

1/4 cup chopped cilantro

La Encrucijada

MEXICO, HIDALGO, DISTRITO FEDERAL (MEXICO CITY), TLAXCALA, PUEBLA, MORELOS

LA ENCRUCIJADA, THE CROSSROADS, SEEMS A PERFECT NAME FOR THIS REGION. All roads, airlines, and commerce pass through here. The Valley of Mexico, the heart of this region, is the cradle of the ancient Aztec empire, and modern-day Mexico City is one of the largest metropolitan areas on the planet. Puebla is the birthplace of mole, the quintessential Mexican dish, and legends cite Tlaxcala as the origin of corn tortillas. In the markets, you will see specialties from all the regions of the country, and the masses of people bustling around reflect the melting pot that is Mexico. In the small towns and villages, you will discover markets and street vendors serving preparations that date to preconquest times; and, if you are lucky enough to be invited into a private home, you may taste family recipes that have been passed down through the centuries, refined and adapted by successive generations. In the metropolitan areas, particularly in Mexico City, or "D.F." (dey-ef-ay), as it is known to most Mexicans, you can visit markets and small restaurants where you may taste traditional fare from around the country; or you may choose to try one of the trendy, upscale eateries that serve contemporary and stylized versions of dishes that were, in the not-too-distant past, disdained by the upper classes as "indigenous food," unfit for sophisticated palates. There is no better place to study the gastronomy of this amazing country.

Chiles en Nogada (Puebla)

CHILE RELLENOS IN WALNUT SAUCE WITH PORK-PICADILLO FILLING

FOR THE FILLING

2 pounds ground pork

Salt and pepper to taste

1 teaspoon ground canela

1 teaspoon ground allspice, toasted

1/4 teaspoon ground cloves

2 cups water

1 onion, cut in quarters

3 bay leaves

2 cloves garlic, smashed

1/2 onion, chopped

2 tablespoons butter

8 roasted plum tomatoes, pureed and strained

1 apple, peeled and finely chopped

2 firm bananas or 1 ripe plantain, chopped

1/4 cup candied cactus fruit or raisins, finely chopped

1 tablespoon sugar

1/2 cup pine nuts or slivered almonds, lightly toasted

THIS IS THE CLASSIC, patriotic national dish that is popular during the month of September—the 16th being Mexico's Independence Day. The dish features the green, red, and white of the Mexican flag. It was reportedly first served to Emperor Maximilian and can be found most of the year in Puebla restaurants.

MAKES 8 SERVINGS

1. For the filling, season the meat with salt, pepper, canela, allspice, and clove; add water, quartered onion, bay leaves, and garlic; simmer until tender; then strain. Remove the onion, bay leaves, and garlic.

2. Sweat (don't brown) the chopped onion in butter in a separate pan until transparent; add the tomato and heat through; then add the fruit and sugar. Season with salt and pepper.

3. Simmer for another 2 minutes, incorporate the meat and pine nuts or almonds into the mixture, and simmer for another few minutes to allow the flavors to blend.

4. For the sauce, blend the walnuts in a food processor with the cream cheese, bread, sherry, sugar, and salt. Gently warm (do not boil). If the walnut sauce is too thick, add a little cream.

5. Stuff the chiles with the filling and heat through in a 350-degree-F oven for about 10 minutes. Place the chiles in a serving dish and cover them with the walnut sauce. Decorate with pomegranate seeds and parsley or cilantro.

FOR THE SAUCE

2 cups shelled walnuts, lightly toasted

1/2 cup cream cheese or unsweetened mascarpone

1 slice bread, soaked in 1/4 cup milk

1/8 cup semidry sherry*

1 tablespoon sugar

salt to taste

Cream

FOR THE CHILE RELLENOS

16 small or 8 large chiles poblanos, roasted, peeled and carefully seeded (see page 23)

*Apple juice may be substituted, but if using, then omit sugar from the recipe.

Mixiotes

SEASONED MEATS STEAMED IN MAGUEY WRAPPERS

MIXIOTES ARE POPULAR throughout central Mexico. They are usually steamed rather than buried in the earth. By tradition, the tough outer leaves of maguey are the preferred wrap for mixiotes; however, banana leaves, baking paper, or foil also work well. This recipe originally called for rabbit, and is delicious that way, but it works equally well with chicken, pork, mutton, or wild game, such as venison or elk. Typically served in individual portions, this recipe can also be prepared in larger quantities to be divided later for serving. Mixiotes may be made several days in advance and then reheated in a steamer or oven before serving.

MAKES 6 TO 8 SERVINGS

1. Slowly cook the bacon on a skillet until most of the fat is rendered. Sauté the onion until slightly browned and add the garlic, cloves, cumin, and canela and cook for 1 more minute.

2. Add the tomatoes, chiles, vinegar, stock or water, and salt and pepper and bring the mixture to a boil; then reduce heat and simmer for about 20 minutes.

3. Puree in a blender until smooth.

4. Place the sauce in a nonreactive container, add the meat, and marinate for a minimum of 2 hours and up to overnight.

5. If using maguey or banana leaves, toast lightly over an open flame to render them more flexible (see page 29).

6. Divide the meat amongst the leaves, paper, or foil, and then divide the sauce the same way.

8 slices of bacon, diced or 3 tablespoons lard or oil

1 large white onion, diced

3 to 4 cloves garlic, coarsely chopped

1 teaspoon whole cloves or allspice

1/2 teaspoon cumin seeds, toasted

2 sticks canela

6 to 8 tomatoes, well charred and skin removed

3 to 4 guajillo or red New Mexico chiles, toasted, seeded, and soaked

2 ancho chiles, toasted, seeded, and soaked

1 to 2 chipotle seco or cascabel chiles, toasted, seeded, and soaked (leave the seeds in for a hotter version)

2 tablespoons vinegar (apple cider, pineapple, or rice)

1 cup chicken or pork stock or water

Salt and pepper to taste

4 pounds meat (skinned rabbit quarters, pork shoulder bone-in steaks, cubed pork, chicken leg and thigh quarters, leg of mutton, or venison)

6 to 8 maguey or banana leaves
(baking paper or foil will also
work)

6 to 8 bay leaves, toasted, or 3 to 4
sprigs of fresh epazote

7. Top each package with a bay leaf or epazote sprig and fold or gather the wrapper and secure to keep the sauce and flavors inside.

8. Place in a steamer and cook for 45 minutes for rabbit or chicken or 1 1/2 hours for pork or game meats.

Note: Mixiote is usually served in the cooking wrapper. Be careful when opening the packets to avoid being burned.

Tortillas de Maíz
CORN TORTILLAS

TORTILLAS ARE THE FOUNDATION of Mexican cooking. In the past, a prospective bride was often required to demonstrate her competency in the art of tortilla making to her future mother-in-law. The natives of Tlaxcala (Cortez's allies against Montezuma) are reputed to have first developed corn tortillas, although there are alternate claims to that honor. Interestingly, Cortez's troops are said to have misnamed the tortilla after mistaking it for the Spanish tortilla, which is a type of omelet. The indigenous tortillas were round and flat in shape and golden brown when cooked on a hot ceramic surface.

If you make your own fresh masa or are fortunate to live where you can buy it, skip the first step. The tortillas may seem a little hard when they first come off the griddle, but they should soften up after they steam for a few minutes with the others.

MAKES 16 TO 20 TORTILLAS

2 cups dry masa harina

1/2 teaspoon salt

1 7/8 cup (approximately) warm water (95 to 115 degrees F)

1. Place the dry ingredients in a mixing bowl and slowly add the water while stirring with a fork until the dough comes together into a ball. Knead the dough several times by hand until smooth. Wrap in plastic and let stand for at least 15 minutes.

2. Preheat a comal, heavy skillet, or griddle to medium-high (350 degrees F).

3. Form some masa into a 1-inch ball and place the ball between two sheets of plastic (a freezer bag split into 2 sheets works well). Flatten in a tortilla press or by hand to about 1/16 inch thick.

4. Peel off the top sheet of plastic and gently transfer the tortilla from the other sheet to your bare palm, invert it over the comal or griddle, and slide it onto the cooking surface. Cook for about 20 to 30 seconds, and

then turn over. Cook for 30 to 45 seconds more and flip over again, pushing down with a spatula several times. Tortillas should puff slightly. Properly cooked tortillas will have light brown speckles.

5. Keep the cooked tortillas in a kitchen towel, tortilla warmer, or cloth napkin to keep warm while cooking others. Serve immediately.

Note: This recipe may be prepared using a food processor. Place the dry ingredients in a bowl fitted with a steel blade. While processor is running slowly, pour the warm water through the feed and process until a smooth dough ball is formed. Proceed as above.

Pepeto México

PORK STEW FROM THE STATE OF MÉXICO

PEPETO IS A SIMPLE and easy-to-prepare hearty soup or stew that makes a satisfying main dish. It is best known in Tonatico, Mexico State. I tasted it in the mercado and asked a few questions. The recipe comes from my memory and the few answers that I did receive. Be careful if you use the hot manzano, güero, or habanero chiles!

MAKES 8 SERVINGS

1. Place the pork in a saucepan with enough water to cover and simmer until tender (about 1 1/2 hours).

2. Skim off the excess fat.

3. Add the chilacayotes and beans and simmer for 15 minutes, then add the epazote, onion, corn, chile, and salt and pepper to taste. Cook 10 more minutes and serve in bowls along with the lime and bread or tortillas.

2 pounds pork shoulder (or Boston butt or beef chuck), cut into 1-inch pieces

2 pounds chilacayote or chayote squash (you may substitute other firm squash or potatoes), peeled, seeded, and sliced

2 pounds fresh or fresh frozen lima or green beans

1 to 2 sprigs epazote

2 medium onions, sliced

4 young cobs of corn, sliced in 3/4-inch-thick rounds

1 or 2 chiles manzanos (rocoto or rocotillo), stemmed, seeded, and sliced (you may substitute habanero, güero, jalapeño, or Fresno)

Salt and pepper to taste

Lime slices and bread or tortillas on the side

Salpicón de Res
SHREDDED BEEF SALAD

A REFRESHING TWIST ON ROAST BEEF, Salpicón de Res may be used as a salad or light lunch course, to top chips for an appetizer, or as a filling for tacos and tostadas. In Oaxaca and the Yucatan, the same method is used for venison. This is a great recipe for leftover roast beef.

MAKES 8 SERVINGS

1. Shred the beef in small strips.

2. Peel and slice the carrots and potatoes in 1/4 x 2-inch pieces and blanch in boiling water. Cool.

3. Toss all of the ingredients together in a bowl and let sit for at least 30 minutes before serving.

3 pounds beef chuck or flank steak, prepared as the recipe for Machaca Norteña (see page 35) through the first half of the recipe*

1 or 2 potatoes

1 or 2 carrots

2 roma tomatoes, seeded and cut in thin strips

2 poblano chiles (or 3 jalapeño chiles or 2 chipotle chiles en adobo), seeded and julienned

1 red or white onion, cut in thin strips and rinsed

5 to 6 radishes, washed and cut into half-moon slices or julienned

Juice of 2 limes

Juice of 1/2 orange (or 1 tablespoon pineapple or cider vinegar)

1/3 cup chopped cilantro

Salt and pepper

2 tablespoons olive or vegetable oil

*You can also use leftover roast beef.

Frijoles de Olla
SLOW-COOKED BLACK BEANS

1 pound dried black beans, sorted
  for rocks, debris, and broken
  beans, then rinsed well with
  cold water

3 quarts cold water

1 medium white onion, roughly
  chopped

1 tablespoon lard or vegetable oil

1 1/2 teaspoons salt

1 or 2 sprigs epazote or
  2 teaspoons dried epazote

OPTIONAL INGREDIENTS

1 to 2 whole chipotle, jalapeño,
  or habanero chiles*

1/2 to 1 toasted, seeded, and
  crumbled ancho, guajillo,
  de arbol, or cascabel chile

1/4 teaspoon toasted cumin

2 to 3 bay leaves, toasted

LITERALLY MEANING "POT BEANS," Frijoles de Olla is the basic preparation for beans in most of Mexico. If you want a simple flavor, stay with the basic recipe and maybe an optional ingredient or two; if you want a more complex flavor like the southern Mexican style, use more of the options. Although this recipe is for black beans, it applies to all colors and varieties of beans. The black bean recipes almost always use epazote, while recipes for other colors of beans usually do not. The recipe tastes good either way. The product of this recipe may be used as the base for other preparations involving beans such as Frijoles Colados Yucateco (see page 189).

MAKES 6 TO 8 SERVINGS

1. Place the beans and water in a large pot. The water should be triple the height of the beans in the pot.

2. Add the onion and the lard and slowly heat to boiling.

3. Reduce heat to barely boiling and cook until the beans are completely cooked through, 1 1/2 to 4 hours depending on the dryness of the beans, the altitude, the pot, and your stove. Beans are done when they have a uniform interior color and soft texture throughout.

4. Add the salt, reserving the epazote (and any optional ingredients desired) until the last 15 to 20 minutes to preserve its flavor. Then add the epazote and optional ingredients.

5. Simmer another 45 minutes to 1 hour, stirring occasionally and adding water if needed to prevent burning. The beans will be very soft and creamy in texture, and the broth will have thickened to some degree.

6. Serve in a bowl and top with desired garnishes.

Note: By leaving the chiles whole, you get a lot of flavor without all of the heat. Beans in Mexico are usually not that hot (picante). If you want them hotter, chop some of the chile at the end of the cooking and mix in until it suits you.

2 to 3 avocado leaves or a generous pinch of ground anise seed

1 or 2 hoja santa or acuyo leaves

1 to 2 teaspoons Mexican oregano, toasted

2 cloves garlic, crushed and peeled

GARNISH
Cheese, Jocoque (see page 45), chopped cilantro, shredded cabbage, sliced radishes, chopped onions, and/or chile rajas

Mole Poblano de Convento
CONVENT-STYLE PUEBLA MOLE

8 ounces chiles mulatos, toasted, deveined, and seeded

12 ounces chiles pasillas or guajillos, toasted, deveined, and seeded

12 ounces chiles anchos, toasted, deveined and seeded

5 medium cloves garlic

1 medium white onion, roughly chopped

1/4 pound pork lard

4 dried-out corn tortillas, torn into large pieces

1 slice crusty bread, pan-toasted

3/8 cup raisins

1 ripe plantain, peeled, sliced, and browned in oil or lard

3/4 cup almonds, lightly toasted

1 to 2 teaspoons ancho chile seeds to taste, toasted

3/8 cup sesame seeds

1/2 teaspoon aniseed, toasted

1/2 teaspoon cumin seeds, toasted

MOLE IS THE PREPARATION MOST OFTEN CITED as the perfect example of the blending of the indigenous and the European cultures and their cooking styles and ingredients. It deftly combines the New World ingredients of chiles, tomatoes, and sometimes chocolate with the exotic spices, nuts, seasonings, and techniques of the Old World.

The legend goes like this: the nuns of the Santa Rosa Convent outside of Puebla de Los Angeles were expecting a visit from either the viceroy or the archbishop and wanted to prepare a meal that would impress him and show him how the two cultures were sharing ideas in the kitchen. An alternate story has Fray Pascual accidentally knocking over a tray of spices into a simmering pot of chile. We will probably never know for sure what happened but still get to enjoy the happy consequences.

The name *mole* comes from the Aztec language Nahuatl and refers more to the process of grinding or pureeing the ingredients than it does to the specific ingredients themselves. Traditionally served with turkey, Mole Poblano de Convento is also good with chicken or for enchiladas.

MAKES 12 SERVINGS

1. Soak the chiles in boiling water until soft. Drain.

2. Fry the garlic and onion in half of the lard until transparent; add the tortilla pieces, plantain, bread, raisins, almonds, chile seeds, half the sesame seeds, aniseed, cumin seeds, cloves, canela, peppercorns, chocolate, and tomato and fry. Add the drained chiles and fry for another few seconds.

3. Puree this mixture in a blender with 3 cups of the broth in which the turkey was cooked, and strain.

4. In an earthenware mole pot, Dutch oven, or heavy sauce pot, heat the rest of the lard; add the sauce, frying for 2 to 3 minutes. Reduce heat and simmer the sauce for 5 minutes, season with salt and sugar and, if necessary, add more caldo as needed. The sauce should be fairly thick.

5. Simmer for 25 to 30 more minutes, add the pieces of turkey, and heat through. Serve in the earthenware pot it was cooked in, garnished with the rest of the toasted sesame seeds.

5 cloves

1 canela stick

6 peppercorns or 1 teaspoon ground black pepper

2 tablets Mexican drinking chocolate or 2 tablespoons cocoa powder and 1 tablespoon sugar

1/2 pound roma tomatoes, well roasted and chopped

1 medium turkey or 2 roasting chickens, cut into serving pieces and cooked in good-quality vegetable stock made from carrot, leek, onion, a stick of celery, parsley, and 1 clove garlic, or in Caldo de Pollo (see page 138)

Salt and sugar to taste

Arroz a la Poblana (blanco)
PUEBLA-STYLE WHITE RICE

THIS RICE SIDE DISH, from the central state of Puebla, is a great foil for seafood, spicy tomato-based sauces, and rich, complex moles. By adding additional vegetables and/or garbanzos or other beans, it can be made into a hearty accompaniment to leftovers or a meatless main course. The milk and broth make it smooth and rich, but the rice may also be prepared using only water as the liquid.

MAKES 6 TO 8 SERVINGS

1. Preheat a heavy saucepan or skillet over high heat; add the oil, then the rice and half of the salt. Stirring constantly, cook the rice until over half of the grains are opaque white and a few of the grains are beginning to slightly brown.

2. Add the carrot, onion, and garlic and continue cooking and stirring until the onion begins to soften.

3. Add the chiles, corn, and the remaining salt; then add the liquids and the cilantro or thyme.

   Note: The mixture will be very hot before you add the liquids. Be very careful to avoid the steam and splattering when the liquid is introduced.

4. Stir well and bring to a full boil. Stir once again and cover tightly.

5. Reduce heat to simmer and leave covered (no peeking) for 15 minutes. Remove from heat and leave cover in place for 10 more minutes.

6. Fluff with a spoon or fork and stir in the sour cream if desired. Serve within 10 to 20 minutes.

3 tablespoons vegetable oil

1 1/2 cups long grain white rice (not converted)

2 teaspoons salt

1 medium carrot, peeled and diced small or sliced in thin half-moon shapes

1 medium red or white onion, cut in thin strips

2 cloves garlic, peeled and crushed (optional)

1 to 2 poblano, Anaheim, or New Mexican green chiles, roasted, peeled, seeded, and cut into 1/4-inch strips

1 1/4 cups corn

1 cup milk or water

2 cups chicken broth or water

1/3 cup coarsely chopped cilantro or 1 tablespoon chopped fresh thyme

1/2 cup sour cream (optional)

Xolostle

CHICKEN IN A RED CHILE SAUCE

I HAVE HEARD THE TERM *XOLOSTLE* applied to other dishes as well, but this version with chicken is the one I have encountered most often. It is simple to make, and the leftovers make great fillings for tacos or other masa-based antojitos. The cascabel chiles give a complex, hot, and nutty flavor to the dish; however, you may freely substitute guajillo, chipotle, ancho, or New Mexican chiles as you like. You should serve it in bowls or dishes that can accommodate the liquid that is produced.

MAKES 6 TO 8 SERVINGS

1. Rinse the chicken pieces, pat dry, and season with salt.

2. Preheat a heavy skillet, add the oil, and brown the chicken pieces well on all sides. Remove from the pan and set aside.

3. In the same pan, add the onions and garlic, and sauté until color begins to develop. Add the cumin and the chile pieces, then the masa harina or flour, stirring well. Cook for about 1 minute; add 1 cup of the cool broth or water. Add vinegar and remove from heat. Stir well to incorporate the masa harina.

4. In a cooking pot, casserole, or Dutch oven, heat the remainder of the broth to boiling. Add the chicken pieces, onion, garlic, chile mixture, and epazote. Bring to a boil, and then reduce the heat and simmer for 35 to 40 minutes until the chicken is fork-tender.

   Note: You may also bake the Xolostle in the oven at 350 degrees F uncovered for 40 to 50 minutes.

5. Serve a piece of the chicken and a generous amount of sauce with white rice, tortillas, and, if you like, chopped cilantro and lime.

*6 to 8 chicken leg and thigh
   quarters*

Salt

1/4 cup vegetable oil or lard

*1 medium white onion,
   cut in thin strips*

*6 cloves garlic, peeled and
   cut in half lengthwise*

Generous pinch of ground cumin

*8 to 10 cascabel chiles, toasted,
   seeded, and torn into small pieces*

*1/4 cup masa harina or
   3 tablespoons all-purpose flour*

2 quarts chicken broth or water

*1 tablespoon mild vinegar
   (pineapple, apple cider, or rice)*

*1 or 2 sprigs fresh epazote or
   1 tablespoon Mexican oregano
   and 2 bay leaves*

*Cilantro, lime, and tortillas
   on the side*

Crema de Cacahuate y Chipotle
PEANUT AND CHIPOTLE CREAM SOUP

I FIRST TASTED THIS SOUP in Cuernavaca in a restaurant whose name I can no longer remember; however, I still remember the flavor of the soup. The combination of peanuts and chipotle is a classic flavor, illustrating the Moorish-African influence in Mexican cuisine.

MAKES 6 TO 8 SERVINGS

1. Fry the onion and garlic in the oil until a light color develops. Remove from the oil.

2. Fry the peanuts in the remaining oil until lightly browned; add the chipotle chiles and cook 1 minute more.

3. Puree the peanuts, chiles, onion, and garlic with the Caldo de Pollo until smooth.

4. Mix the puree with the cream and the wine and simmer over medium-low heat for 20 to 30 minutes.

5. Add salt to taste. Garnish with cheese and toasted oregano, marjoram, or cilantro and serve hot. Or this dish may be served as a chilled soup with the cheese omitted.

1/2 white onion, coarsely chopped

4 to 5 cloves garlic, peeled

2 to 3 tablespoons vegetable oil

1/2 pound skinless peanuts

2 to 3 chipotle chiles en adobo plus 1 tablespoon of the juice from the canned chiles

2 cups Caldo de Pollo (see page 138)

1 cup light cream (or 1/2 cup milk with 1/2 cup sour cream or Jocoque)

1 cup dry white wine or 1 tablespoon cider vinegar and 1/2 cup additional chicken stock

Salt to taste (be careful if using salted peanuts)

1/2 cup cheese for garnish (asadero, fresco, cotija, fontina, or Monterey Jack)

1 to 2 tablespoons toasted Mexican oregano, fresh sweet marjoram, or cilantro for garnish

Caldo de Pollo
CHICKEN BROTH

Bones from 2 to 3 roasted chickens,
 broken into 4 or 5 pieces

2 medium onions, quartered

3 to 4 carrots, peeled
 and roughly chopped

3 cloves garlic, peeled

3 ribs celery, cut into 3-inch
 sections

4 to 5 bay leaves, toasted

1 to 2 sprigs each fresh marjoram,
 thyme, epazote, parsley, and
 cilantro

1 teaspoon allspice, toasted

2 teaspoons whole black
 peppercorns, lightly toasted

2 tablespoons salt

Enough cold water to cover the
 bones and aromatics (about 8
 to 10 quarts)

THIS BROTH IS USED AS A BASE for many soups, stews, sauces, and rice dishes. The only essential ingredient is the chicken bones; however, the aromatics do add a certain depth of flavor. You may pick and choose from the seasonings as availability dictates or according to your personal tastes. You can make this recipe by first starting with only 1 or 2 whole chickens. Cook the chicken(s) in the liquid with or without the aromatics. Remove the cooked chickens from the broth, cool, then remove the skin and the cooked meat to use in another recipe. Skim any excess fat from the broth and return the bones to the broth to continue preparing the caldo.

The broth freezes well. If you put it in ice cube trays and then place the cubes in plastic bags to keep in the freezer, you can easily get the quantities that you need for a particular recipe.

MAKES ABOUT 1 TO 1 1/2 GALLONS

1. Place all of the ingredients in a stockpot or large kettle and slowly bring to a boil. Occasionally skim the surface to remove any foam or small particles.

2. Boil for 15 minutes, and then remove from heat for 15 to 20 minutes. Add 1 quart very cold water and let sit for 5 more minutes.

3. Without stirring, skim again to remove any surface scum, particles, or fat.

4. Reheat to a slow boil and cook for 1 1/2 to 2 hours. If the level of the liquid drops below the top of the bones, add more cold water as needed and proceed with cooking.

5. Remove from heat and cool for 20 to 30 minutes.

6. Remove the bones and strain liquid through a sieve or colander lined with cheesecloth.

7. Chill the strained broth completely and skim the fat from the surface.

   Note: At this point, you may reheat the caldo and reduce by 1/3 to concentrate the flavors or reduce even more to conserve space when storing.

Caldo de Res
BEEF BROTH

2 to 3 pounds beef bones

2 medium onions, quartered

3 to 4 carrots, peeled
    and roughly chopped

8 cloves garlic, peeled

3 ribs celery, cut into 3-inch
    sections

6 to 7 bay leaves, toasted

1 to 2 sprigs each fresh marjoram,
    thyme, and epazote

1 tablespoon whole black
    peppercorns, lightly toasted

2 tablespoons salt

Enough cold water to cover
    the bones and aromatics
    (about 8 to 10 quarts)

NOT USED AS FREQUENTLY AS CALDO DE POLLO, Caldo de Res is as versatile and may be substituted. If you are short on beef bones, you may boil bone-in chuck roast or beef shanks and use the meat in another recipe. After removing the meat, just return the bones to the pot and proceed.

MAKES 1 TO 1 1/2 GALLONS

1. Place all of the ingredients in a stockpot or large kettle and slowly bring to a boil. Occasionally skim the surface to remove any foam or small particles. (For more depth of flavor and color, first roast the bones for 30 to 40 minutes in a 375-degree-F oven.)

2. Boil for 15 minutes, and then remove from heat for 15 to 20 minutes. Add 1 quart very cold water and let sit for 5 more minutes.

3. Without stirring, skim again to remove any surface scum, particles, or fat.

4. Reheat to a slow boil and cook for 1 1/2 to 2 hours. If the level of the liquid drops below the top of the bones, add more cold water as needed and proceed with cooking.

5. Remove from heat and cool for 20 to 30 minutes.

6. Remove the bones and strain liquid through a sieve or colander lined with cheesecloth.

7. Chill the strained broth completely and skim the fat from the surface.

   Note: At this point, you may reheat the caldo and reduce by 1/3 to concentrate the flavors or reduce even more to conserve space when storing.

Caldo de Pescado

FISH BROTH

LIKE CALDO DE POLLO, this broth is used as a base for many soups, stews, sauces, and rice dishes. However, the cooking time is less and there are a few changes in the aromatics.

MAKES 5 QUARTS

1. Place all of the ingredients except the limes or lemons and white wine in a stockpot or large kettle and slowly bring to a boil. Occasionally skim the surface to remove any foam or small particles.

2. Boil for 5 minutes, and then remove from heat for 15 to 20 minutes. Add 1 quart very cold water and let sit for 5 more minutes.

3. Without stirring, skim again to remove any surface scum, particles, or fat. Add the limes or lemons and the wine if using.

4. Reheat and simmer (do not boil) for 30 to 45 minutes. Remove from heat and cool for 20 to 30 minutes.

5. Remove the bones and strain liquid through a sieve or colander lined with cheesecloth.

6. Chill the strained broth completely and skim the fat from the surface.

   Note: At this point, you may reheat the caldo to boiling and reduce by no more than 1/3 to concentrate the flavors.

2 to 3 pounds fish bones, fish heads, and/or shrimp, crab, and lobster shells

2 medium onions, quartered

3 to 4 carrots, peeled and roughly chopped

3 ribs celery, cut in 3-inch sections

3 to 4 bay leaves, toasted

1 to 2 sprigs each thyme, epazote, parsley, and cilantro

1 teaspoon allspice, toasted

1 teaspoon coriander seeds, toasted

1/2 teaspoon whole cloves

1 teaspoon whole black peppercorns, lightly toasted

2 tablespoons salt

Enough cold water to cover the bones and aromatics (about 6 quarts)

2 to 3 limes or lemons, cut in half

2 cups dry white wine (optional)

Salsa Fresca

THIS UBIQUITOUS SALSA is often called *Salsa Mexicana* both because it is a typical salsa throughout the country and because it has the red, green, and white colors of the Mexican flag. In the Yucatan and Quintana Roo, when it is made with habanero instead of jalapeño chiles, it is called *xni-pec* (shnee-peck), which is the Mayan word for a dog's wet nose; a runny nose is one of the side effects you may experience with that fiery version of this salsa.

MAKES ABOUT 3 CUPS

1. Put the tomatoes, garlic, onion, lime juice, vinegar, chiles, and salt to taste in a bowl and mix well. You may coarsely puree this mixture in a food processor, or you can leave the ingredients intact for more texture. Taste after 10 minutes and adjust the chiles and lime juice to suit your taste.

2. Add the cilantro. (The cilantro is reserved until after the adjustment so that it does not mask the flavors of the chile and the lime. It takes about 10 minutes for the interaction of the lime's acidity and the chile's heat to stabilize.)

3. Add the olive oil, if desired. It will make the salsa shiny, add a bit of flavor, and help to preserve it. Let the mixture sit for 30 minutes to allow the flavors to develop. The ideal serving temperature is 55 to 60 degrees F, so don't serve it directly from the refrigerator.

4 to 5 ripe plum tomatoes, diced into 1/4-inch cubes

1/4 teaspoon finely minced garlic (optional)

1/2 cup finely chopped red or white onion, rinsed (see page 19)

1/8 cup fresh lime juice

2 tablespoons mild vinegar (apple cider or rice)

2 or 3 fresh jalapeño or serrano chiles, seeded (if jalapeño), and finely chopped

Salt to taste

1/4 cup coarsely chopped cilantro

1 tablespoon olive oil (optional)

Salsa Verde
GREEN TAQUERIA-STYLE SAUCE

THIS IS A TYPICAL VERSION of a typical salsa. This salsa is great on tacos and with grilled meats, empanadas, quesadillas, and chips. Variations are created by boiling the ingredients or making it raw, pureed, or liquefied. The lemony flavor of the tomatillos is a good contrast to rich or fatty foods.

MAKES ABOUT 2 CUPS

1. Lightly char the tomatillos on a comal or in a heavy skillet, along with the garlic, chiles, and onion for about 5 to 6 minutes or until they are somewhat browned and caramelized (see techniques chapter). The tomatillos should retain some of their bright green color. Cool.

2. Coarsely chop the cilantro leaves, garlic, onion, and chiles.

3. Place the tomatillos and the roasted onion, garlic, and chiles in a blender or food processor and blend, adding a little water if necessary. The sauce should be thick.

4. Pour the sauce into a bowl. Add cilantro, lime juice, and sugar (if the salsa is too tart), and season with salt to taste.

1 dozen tomatillos, husked and rinsed (see page 27)

6 cloves garlic, peeled

3 to 4 serrano chiles, stems removed (or jalapeño chiles with seeds removed for a milder salsa)

1 small white onion, sliced in 3 rounds

1 bunch fresh cilantro

Juice of 1/2 lime

1/2 teaspoon sugar (if needed to balance the acidity)

Salt to taste

El Centro Colonial

GUANAJUATO, ZACATECAS, SAN LUIS POTOSI, GUADALAJARA, AGUASCALIENTES, EASTERN JALISCO, AND MICHOACÁN

THE COLONIAL PERIOD IN MEXICAN HISTORY, from the mid-sixteenth century to the early nineteenth century, had a profound impact on religion, architecture, politics, culture, and gastronomy that is still very evident today. Although colonial influences remain in all of the country, they are the most evident in the states of the central highlands. Mining and agriculture dictated the locations of many cities and towns. The riches generated by the prolific mining operations are still evident; massive, elaborately decorated churches and cathedrals as well as colonial style public structures abound. The landscape ranges from lush forested mountains to parched, arid llanos (high desert flatlands) with fertile plains and cattle-grazing lands in between.

The food also bears the unmistakable stamp of the Spanish colonial influence; however, the indigenous spirit remains. Influenced by commercial agriculture and cattle ranching, the cuisine emphasizes meat and corn, but rustic and sometimes exotic ingredients such as wild herbs, wild game, freshwater fish, insects, fruits, and cactus are also popular.

Uchepos
MICHOACÁN-STYLE SWEET CORN TAMALES

6 large, tender ears of corn

1/2 cup butter

3 tablespoons sugar

1 teaspoon salt

1 teaspoon baking soda

cornhusk

SIMILAR TO TAMALES DE ELOTES, custard-like uchepos should be made when sweet corn is at its peak. The sweet corn in Mexico is a little firmer and contains more starch than the north-of-the-border variety. I often add about 2 tablespoons of masa harina or 2 teaspoons of cornstarch to help thicken the uchepos. To make savory Uchepos, omit the sugar, add mild chiles, epazote, or cilantro, and a cheese such as cotija or queso fresco. Uchepos are good served with breakfast or as an appetizer or side dish.

MAKES 4 SERVINGS

1. Carefully husk and de-silk the corn, saving the leaves to wrap the tamales.

2. Cut the corn off the cob and finely grind the kernels in a food processor.

3. Beat the butter with the sugar and salt until fluffy, and mix with the ground corn kernels and baking soda.

4. Spoon the mixture into the cornhusks. Wrap them to make small tamales and cook in a steamer for 30 to 40 minutes or until the leaves come away easily. Alternatively, place them in a pressure cooker for 12 minutes. Serve with breakfast or as an appetizer or side dish.

Tamales de Muerto Querétaro
BLUE CORN TAMALES WITH PORK

EARTHY-TASTING, DARK BLUISH-GREY MASA with the slightly smoky, deep, dried-fruit flavor of ancho chiles and the salty sharpness of cotija cheese, these tamales are traditionally served to commemorate the Day of the Dead in Querétaro. They are unique to the area and are a bit unusual in that the masa is first filled, then rolled into a cylinder, chilled, and sliced. The slices are then placed in the cornhusk to be steamed. They are good anytime and would go well with Lomo de Cerdo Negro a la Querétaro (see page 159).

MAKES 18 TO 20 TAMALES

1. For the masa, thoroughly mix the dry masa and the warm water, cover, and let sit for 20 to 30 minutes.

2. For the dough, beat the lard well until creamy and white, and then add the rehydrated masa, baking powder, broth, and salt in increments. Continue beating until a small piece of dough floats in a glass of cold water.

3. Soak the cornhusks in water for 2 hours, then shake them dry.

4. For the filling, after the chiles have been soaked, blend them with the onions and garlic and a little of the water they have been soaked in.

5. Heat the lard in a frying pan, then strain the chile mixture into the pan. Add the salt and lightly fry until mixture is thickened. Add the grated cheese and remove from the heat.

FOR THE MASA
2 pounds dry blue corn masa

2 cups warm water

FOR TAMALE DOUGH
1 pound pork lard

2 pounds rehydrated blue corn masa

1 tablespoon baking powder

1 cup chicken broth

Salt to taste

Dry cornhusks

FOR THE FILLING

12 ancho chiles, deveined, toasted, and soaked in very hot water

2 medium onions

1 clove garlic

1 ounce pork lard

Salt to taste

1 1/4 cups grated hard cheese such as cotija

6. Wet a cloth napkin or smooth towel, squeeze out, and lay flat. Spread the dough over this about 3/8 inch thick, then spoon a layer of filling over the dough. Roll up the dough with the towel, forming a cylinder, and chill, covered, for 15 minutes. Cut into slices 3/4 inch thick. Place the rolled and sliced dough with filling in the cornhusks. Wrap up like tamales, stack upright in a steamer, and steam for an hour until the husk comes away easily from the masa.

Churipo

COUNTRY-STYLE PORK, BEEF, AND CHICKEN STEW

THIS RICH AND HEARTY STEW is often prepared outdoors in the small villages around Lake Pátzcuaro in Michoacán. Before the Spanish conquest, the indigenous peoples of the area prepared a similar concoction using wild game, gathered herbs, and cultivated vegetables.

MAKES 6 TO 8 SERVINGS

1. Season the meats with salt and pepper.

2. Puree the tomato, chiles, and garlic together.

3. In a preheated heavy soup kettle or pot, place the oil and the pork and beef, stirring occasionally until the meat is browned. Add the onion and cook for 2 to 3 minutes more. Add the tomato-chile puree and cook 1 more minute, stirring constantly.

4. Add the caldo or water, and bring to a boil. Lower heat to a slow boil, and cook for 30 to 45 minutes until the meat is almost tender. Add the chicken and continue cooking for 20 minutes longer.

5. Add the carrots and cook for 15 minutes, then add the remaining vegetables and herbs. Cook until the vegetables are done (15 to 20 minutes), remove the herbs, and adjust the seasonings to taste.

1 1/2 cups beef-stew meat in bite-sized chunks

1 1/2 cups pork-stew meat in bite-sized chunks

1 1/2 cups skinless chicken dark meat in bite-sized chunks

Salt and pepper

3 to 4 roma tomatoes, roasted until lightly blackened

2 to 3 ancho or mulato chiles, toasted, stemmed, seeded, and soaked (see page 25)

3 cloves garlic, pan-roasted until golden brown (see page 23)

1 to 2 tablespoons vegetable oil

1 medium white onion, sliced in 1/4-inch strips

2 1/2 quarts Caldo de Pollo or Caldo de Res (see pages 138, 140) or water

2 to 3 carrots, peeled and sliced in 1/8-inch-thick half moons

1 cup green beans

1 cup peas

1 pound zucchini or yellow summer squash, sliced into 1/4-inch-thick half moons

1 sprig epazote or 1 sprig each thyme and marjoram

Sopa de Tomate con Fideos
TOMATO SOUP WITH VERMICELLI

THIS IS NOT THE DISH most of us would think of when considering Mexican cooking. However, while traveling around the country, I encountered this soup in many different places—from private homes and large cafeterias to tiny fondas (restaurants) serving fast food. As mundane as the simple ingredients seem, this is a comforting and satisfying course when prepared using good technique. You may omit the chile in this recipe and serve with a salsa to accompany instead.

MAKES 4 TO 6 SERVINGS

1. Slow-roast the tomatoes, onion, and garlic on a comal until tomatoes are slightly blackened and onion and garlic are golden brown. Puree tomatoes, onion, garlic, chile, and epazote in a blender with 1 cup of the caldo.

2. In a preheated heavy saucepan or skillet, add the oil and then the fideos or vermicelli. Fry, stirring frequently until all of the pasta is golden brown.

3. Add the tomato puree and continue frying for 2 minutes while constantly stirring.

4. Add the remaining caldo and the vinegar carefully to minimize splattering. Season with salt and pepper. Bring to a boil, reduce to simmer, and cook for 12 minutes. Serve immediately, garnished with fresh limes and grated cheese.

1 pound ripe tomatoes (12 ounces canned whole tomatoes may be substituted but they cannot be roasted)

1 medium white onion, sliced in 1/2-inch-thick rounds

5 cloves garlic, peeled

1 ancho chile, toasted, seeded, and soaked until soft (you may add or substitute chipotle seco or guajillo, cascabel, New Mexico red, or other chiles to suit your taste)

3 to 4 epazote leaves (or the leaves from a sprig of fresh thyme or marjoram), optional

2 tablespoons vegetable oil

16 ounces Mexican fideos or thin vermicelli, broken into 1-inch pieces

6 cups Caldo de Pollo (see page 138) or water

Dash of mild vinegar

Salt and pepper to taste

Quesadillas de Maíz con Garbanzos Frescos o Flor de Calabaza

CORN TURNOVERS WITH FRESH GARBANZO OR SQUASH-BLOSSOM FILLING

QUESADILLAS ARE ONE OF THE MANY CORN MASA SNACKS found in Mexico. This recipe uses uncooked masa, which is folded around the filling and then cooked on a comal, griddle, or frying pan. Quesadillas may be filled with just about anything you can think of and often, as the name implies, cheese is involved. Other fillings might include chile strips, picadillo, carnitas, cochinita pibil, shredded chicken, huitlacoche (corn fungus), smoked fish, crab, epazote, beans, eggs, prickly pear cactus, mushrooms, potatoes, and so on. The list is only limited by your imagination.

MAKES 12 TO 14 LARGE OR ABOUT 2 DOZEN SMALL QUESADILLAS

FOR THE QUESADILLAS

1. Place the masa harina and salt in a mixing bowl and slowly add the water and the lard or shortening while stirring with a fork until the dough comes together into a ball. Knead the dough several times by hand until smooth. Wrap in plastic and let stand for at least 15 minutes.

2. Preheat a comal, heavy skillet, or griddle to medium-high (350 degrees F).

3. Form some masa into a 1 1/2-inch ball (for large quesadillas) and place the ball between 2 sheets of plastic (a freezer bag split into 2 sheets works well). Flatten in a tortilla press or by hand to about 1/8 inch thick.

4. Place the masa (between the 2 sheets of plastic) in one open hand and carefully peel off the top sheet of plastic.

5. Place about 2 tablespoons of filling in the center, and then carefully fold the masa to create a half-moon shape with the filling encased. (Try not to let the filling reach the edges so that a better seal is made.) Seal the edges with your fingers or with a fork.

QUESADILLAS

2 cups dry masa harina

1/2 teaspoon salt

1 7/8 cup (approximately) warm water (95 to 115 degrees F)

2 tablespoons pork lard or vegetable shortening

2 1/2 to 3 cups of your favorite filling

GARBANZO FILLING

2 cups shelled fresh or dry garbanzo beans, cooked

1 clove garlic, peeled

1 serrano or jalapeño chile, stemmed, seeded, and roughly chopped

1 green onion (white portion), chopped

1 to 2 tablespoons cilantro or epazote, chopped

1 teaspoon fresh lime juice

Salt and pepper

6 to 8 ounces asadero, quesadilla, queso fresco, or Monterrey jack cheese, crumbled, shredded, or sliced

SQUASH-BLOSSOM FILLING

2 tablespoons butter or olive oil

1 to 2 serrano or jalapeño chiles, thinly sliced (or 1 poblano or New Mexican green chile, roasted, peeled, and cut into strips)

2 to 3 green onions, cut in 1-inch sections and finely julienned

Salt and pepper

14 to 18 fresh squash or pumpkin blossoms, stem, stamen, and pistil removed, julienned in 1/4-inch strips

25 to 30 fresh oregano (or marjoram leaves, 1/8 cup chopped cilantro, or 5 to 7 fresh epazote leaves, julienned)

1 cup Jocoque (see page 45) (or sour cream or 8 ounces mild cheese)

Salsa on the side

6. Place on a comal or griddle (you may brush the comal or griddle with oil to make the quesadilla brown more if you like), or fry in oil.

7. Cook until the quesadilla is golden brown on one side and turn over to cook the other. Place on paper towels and cover with a kitchen towel to keep warm. Follow the same process for the remaining ingredients.

FOR THE GARBANZO FILLING

1. Place all of the ingredients, except the cheese and salsa or jocoque, in a molcajete or food processor. Blend to a smooth consistency.

2. Place some of the cheese on each tortilla, followed by 1 to 2 tablespoons of the garbanzo puree.

3. Serve with salsa and/or jocoque on the side.

FOR THE SQUASH-BLOSSOM FILLING

1. Preheat a sauté pan and a comal, griddle, or fryer.

2. Place the butter or olive oil in the pan, add the chiles and sauté for about 1 minute.

3. Add the green onions and continue for 30 seconds more. Season with salt and pepper and add the squash or pumpkin blossoms and herbs. Cook about 1 minute until the onions begin to soften.

4. Place 1 tablespoon of the jocoque on each tortilla, followed by 1 to 2 tablespoons of the squash-blossom mixture.

5. Serve with salsa.

Pozole Estilo de Michoacán
HOMINY AND PORK STEW

16 to 24 ounces fresh or frozen pozole (or 1 1/2 cups dry pozole that has been soaked in cool water for 8 to 12 hours, then drained)

2 1/2 pounds pork-stew meat or pork-shoulder meat cut into 1-inch cubes

2 tablespoons pork lard or vegetable oil

1 medium white onion, diced

3 cloves garlic, coarsely chopped

Generous pinch of cumin

1 to 2 tablespoons toasted Mexican oregano

2 bay leaves, toasted

Pinch of ground cloves or allspice

1 ancho chile and 1 guajillo chile, toasted, stemmed, seeded, and coarsely chopped

1 chipotle chile en adobe, pureed (optional)

Water or pork broth as needed

Salt to taste

Pozole is popular in many Latin American countries. It is made from corn that is treated with the mineral lime and then cooked with spices and often meat to make a hearty soup or stew. The lime treatment enhances the nutritional value of the corn and changes its flavor.

In the markets and several other street locations in Morelia, the capital of the state of Michoacán, you can find some of the best pozole in Mexico. That is not to say that there are not other great versions, but this one typifies for me what pozole is all about.

MAKES 6 TO 8 SERVINGS

1. Gently boil the pozole in enough water to cover for 25 to 40 minutes. The kernels will just begin to open up or "blossom."

2. In a separate skillet, salt and brown the pork well in the lard or vegetable oil. Remove from the pan and lightly brown the onion and garlic.

3. Return the pork to the pan and add the spices, the chopped chiles, and chile puree if using.

4. Stir well and fry for about 3 minutes, then add water or broth to 1 inch above the meat.

5. Bring to a boil, cover, and reduce heat. Simmer 25 to 35 minutes until the meat begins to get tender.

6. Combine with the pozole and simmer for 25 to 40 minutes more until meat is very tender.

7. Serve this stew topped with shredded cabbage, chopped onions, radishes, fresh limes, cilantro, or toasted oregano, toasted ground chile powder, and cotija or other sharp, crumbly cheese for garnish.

Lomo de Cerdo Negro a la Querétaro
PORK LOIN WITH BLACK PRUNE SAUCE

THIS IS A SIMPLE PREPARATION FOR PORK showing the Spanish colonial influence in the cooking of Querétaro. It is rich, sweet, and only a little spicy. The Lomo makes a great main dish for a formal dinner or a not-too-spicy addition to an elaborate Mexican buffet. The leftovers may be shredded to use for tacos, empanada filling, on tostadas, and so on.

MAKES 4 TO 6 SERVINGS

1. Rub the salt, pepper, and chile powder over the tenderloin and set aside for at least 2 hours.

2. Fry the pork in the butter and oil, browning on all sides. When the meat is lightly browned, add the onion, garlic, and jalapeños and sauté until soft.

3. Add the prunes, hot water or Caldo de Pollo, and salt to taste. Cover tightly and simmer until tender.

4. Slice meat and top with the sauce that is formed during cooking. Garnish with parsley, cilantro, or oregano.

Note: This dish can also be made in a pressure cooker.

Salt, pepper, and ground chile powder to taste

2 1/2 pounds pork tenderloin or center-cut pork loin split in half lengthwise, trimmed of all fat

1/2 stick butter

2 tablespoons vegetable oil

1 large onion, quartered, with the layers separated

2 cloves garlic, finely chopped

2 jalapeños, stemmed, seeded, deveined, and cut into 1/8-inch strips

1/2 cup prunes, pitted and roughly chopped

1 cup hot water or Caldo de Pollo (see page 138)

Salt to taste

Chopped parsley, cilantro, or oregano, for garnish

Pescado Pátzcuaro

SOUSED WHITEFISH

PÁTZCUARO IS A QUAINT AND SERENE TILE-ROOFED COLONIAL TOWN in the highlands of central Michoacán, an hour from Morelia. It is situated next to a picturesque lake of the same name at about 7,000 feet elevation. The indigenous Purechepos of the area are known for their preparations of the white, perch-like fish of the lake. This soused or pickled style is similar to the Pescado en Escabeche of the Yucatán. Both recipes exhibit Mediterranean influence.

MAKES 8 SERVINGS

1. Place enough salted water in a pan to cook the fish. Bring to a boil. Fold the fish fillets in half with the skin facing outwards and place each one in the pan of boiling water. Press the fish with a wooden spoon to make sure the two halves stick together, and gently boil for 2 to 3 minutes. Lift out of the pan, remove skin, and place all eight fish in a nonreactive dish, making sure they do not overlap. Note: You may also use bamboo skewers or large toothpicks to keep the fillets together after folding.

2. Reserve the water the fish was cooked in.

3. For the souse, fry the garlic in the hot oil until brown, then remove garlic and set aside. Add the onions and fry until transparent. Remove from heat and allow to cool slightly.

4. Add the remaining ingredients and fried garlic, then strain 2 cups of the water used for cooking the fish into the mixture. Simmer for 20 minutes and then pour over the fish and set aside to cool. This dish tastes better when prepared the night before.

5. Serve cool or at room temperature as a salad or appetizer course or mix with rice as a lunch or supper dish. The soused fish is also good as a filling for empanadas, tacos, or gorditas.

Salted water

8 skin-on Pátzcuaro whitefish fillets (or perch, tilapia, bass, trout, or other mild freshwater fish)

1 head of garlic, separated into cloves and peeled

1/2 cup corn oil

1/2 cup olive oil

2 large onions, sliced

1 1/2 cups vinegar (pineapple, apple cider, rice, or white)

1 1/2 cups orange juice

5 bay leaves, toasted

1 sprig thyme

1 sprig marjoram

5 peppercorns

5 small, whole, dried red chiles (like pequin, pico de pájaro, japoneses, or chiltepin), toasted*

Salt to taste

*You can substitute 2 fresh chile manzanos or 1 chile habanero, stemmed, seeded, and cut into strips.

Elotes Asados
GRILLED CORN ON THE COB

6 ears fresh corn with husk (I prefer white corn but whatever is
freshest is always the best)

OPTIONAL ACCOMPANIMENTS

Leaves from 1 sprig fresh epazote
(approximately 2 tablespoons),
chopped

Fresh thyme, marjoram, oregano,
or cilantro, or any combination of the four

Toasted Mexican oregano

Cotija cheese, crumbled

1 tablespoon red chile powder (I
prefer New Mexican, guajillo,
cascabel, or chipotle for a hot
flavor and ancho for a mild
flavor)

Garlic herb butter (made with butter, roasted garlic, roasted green
chiles, jalapeño, and fresh
herbs)

GRILLED CORN ON THE COB is one of my favorite street snacks. Another example of an uncomplicated food, simply prepared, that is hard to improve upon, corn on the cob is usually sold by vendors on the plazas or in the markets of many cities, towns, and villages throughout Mexico. I have found it equally enjoyable on a street corner on a crisp, cool, autumn evening in northern Chihuahua; sitting on a bench in the zócalo (central plaza) on a steamy tropical evening in Palenque, Chiapas; or on a summer evening along the Rio Grande in northern New Mexico where I live. Young white field corn is used in Mexico; it is a little chewier and starchier than the sweet corn available north of the border. But either variety is delicious when prepared using the following method.

MAKES 6 SERVINGS

1. Cut the silk that is on the outside of the husk, if you like. Do not open the cornhusk, soak it, or remove the inner silk.

2. Preheat a wood, charcoal, or gas grill or broiler to high, or oven to 450 degrees F.

3. Begin cooking the ears. For the grill or broiler, cook the corn, rotating often, until the outer husks are well charred and the corn kernels give a little when squeezed. This takes about 7 to 10 minutes. For the oven, place the corn on the center rack and bake, rotating 3 or 4 times, until the outer husks are slightly brown and crispy and the corn kernels give a little when squeezed. This takes about 15 to 18 minutes.

Chipotle mayonnaise (made by combining chopped chiles and/or garlic with mayonnaise, a few drops of lime juice, and herbs)

1 or 2 limes, cut into wedges, for squeezing

3 tablespoons pumpkin seeds, toasted and ground

Salt and pepper to taste

4. Allow the ears to steam in their husks for about 5 or 6 minutes, and then remove the husks. The silk will remove easily while husking after the corn is roasted. Serve immediately.

Note: If you want to prepare the corn ahead of time, cook about 20 percent less and then reheat for a few minutes before husking and serving.

5. Serve with your choice of accompaniments or use your own imagination.

Cajeta de Celaya
CARAMEL SAUCE

CELAYA, IN THE COLONIAL HIGHLANDS of Guanajuato State, is renowned throughout Mexico for its caramel. Caramel confections are offered in the market, in many shops around the city, and even at the bus depot. This recipe creates a creamy caramel sauce that is great on ice cream, as a glazing for pastries, in milk shakes, and on many other foods.

MAKES 1 QUART

1 quart whole goat's milk (or 1 quart heavy cream [cow's], or 2 15-ounce cans goat's milk)

1 cup sugar

1/4 teaspoon baking soda

Dash of salt

1 tablespoon premium vanilla extract

1. Place all of the ingredients except the vanilla in a heavy saucepan and whisk well to combine.

2. Heat to boiling and then reduce heat to just below boiling, stirring occasionally.

3. Continue reducing heat until a golden brown thick sauce is formed. During the latter stages of reduction, you will need to stir frequently and continue lowering the heat to prevent burning.

4. Add the vanilla and stir well to blend.

5. Cool completely and then store. Cajeta keeps well in the refrigerator for several months.

Carnitas

BRAISED, FRIED, AND SHREDDED PORK

1 onion, diced

6 cloves garlic, peeled

2 cups Caldo de Pollo (see page 138), pork broth or water

1 1/2 cups (12-ounce can) cola or 1 cup milk

Several sprigs of fresh thyme and sweet marjoram or 2 teaspoons toasted Mexican oregano

4 bay leaves, toasted

6 to 8 whole allspice or cloves (optional)

1 to 2 canela sticks (optional)

1 to 2 chipotle chiles en adobo, chopped (optional)

LITERALLY MEANING "LITTLE MEATS," carnitas are prepared using a method of cooking pork common throughout Mexico but most famous in Michoacán. Although they are fairly simple to make, I have encountered many recipes from cooks all around Mexico and in the United States. Here I have created my own from what I consider the best of them.

You will notice one ingredient, cola, that is somewhat unusual, although not at all rare. The preferred brand is the one most commonly consumed in Mexico and I believe, most of the world. I will let you decide which one it is. This variation is clearly a twentieth-century innovation. Recipes that are more traditional use milk to achieve the caramelization that cola produces so easily. The acidity and sweetness of the soft drink provides an important contrast to the fatty richness of the meat.

Carnitas may be served as a main dish accompanied by tortillas, salsa, guacamole, beans and/or rice. It is also used as a filling for tacos, burritos, tortas, empanadas, gorditas, and so on. My version is slightly less fatty than the traditional recipe because it is baked rather than submersed in lard and fried. Nevertheless, carnitas cannot be a low-fat dish since the rich pork fat is an important part of the flavor.

MAKES 8 TO 10 SERVINGS

1. In a heavy roasting pan (that is small enough that the meat will be loosely touching but not tightly packed), place the onion, garlic, Caldo de Pollo, cola or milk, herbs, canela, and chiles if using and mix to combine.

2. Season the meat with salt and pepper and brown in the lard in a hot skillet.

3. Place the meat in the roaster along with the whole oranges, spooning some of the liquid over the meat to coat it.

4. Bake at 350 degrees F, loosely covered, checking occasionally to ensure that there is still some liquid. If it becomes too dry, add more caldo or water. Halfway through the baking, turn over the

5- to 7-pound Boston butt or pork arm roast, cut into fist-sized chunks (or boneless pork loin rubbed with a thin coating of pork lard after cutting)

Salt and pepper

4 tablespoons pork lard

2 small oranges or tangerines

chunks of meat. Bake for 2 1/2 to 3 1/2 hours until it becomes fall-apart tender.

5. Remove the meat from pan and cool sufficiently to allow handling, then shred with a fork.

6. Cut the oranges in half and squeeze the juice into the pan.

7. Remove the bay leaves, canela, and herbs, and place the shredded meat in the cooking juices, mixing well.

8. Raise the oven temperature to 400 degrees F, then bake, uncovered, stirring occasionally, until the liquid is absorbed and the meat is well browned.

Barbacoa
MARINATED, SLOW-COOKED MEAT

THIS POPULAR MEXICAN METHOD OF SLOW-COOKING MEATS (typically lamb or kid, but pork, chicken, and beef are also used) is commonly used in the central areas, most famously Hidalgo.

The word *barbacoa* originated in the Caribbean and is probably of the same origin as the North American word *barbecue*. Barbacoa refers to a slow pit-cooked process in which the meat is marinated and then wrapped in leaves (usually maguey, an agave plant, but banana leaves with avocado leaves or hoja santa for flavor are used in the south) and then buried in a pit where a fire has burned for some time. Often a pot of vegetables and broth is placed under the meat in the pit to catch the drippings. This soup, which is considered a fine delicacy, is then served with the meat, along with fresh tortillas and condiments.

Burying the maguey-wrapped meat in an outdoor pit is absolutely the best way to prepare this dish, and if you are adventurous you may want to try it, but the alternative methods used in this recipe are very good and are becoming common in Mexico.

MAKES 10 TO 15 SERVINGS

1. For the marinade, first toast the chiles on a comal or heavy skillet, cool slightly, then remove the stems and seeds. Place in the hot water, using a weight if needed to keep the chiles covered; soak for 20 minutes, then strain, reserving the water. Place the chiles in a blender with the remaining marinade ingredients and half of the soaking water. Puree until smooth (add more of the soaking water if needed to make a paste the consistency of very thick spaghetti sauce).

FOR THE MARINADE

8 to 10 dry guajillo chiles (or New Mexican or California red chiles)

4 to 5 ancho chiles

2 1/4 cups very hot (but not boiling) water

8 cloves garlic, peeled

1/2 medium white onion, roughly chopped

1 tablespoon dried, toasted Mexican oregano

1 ounce fresh epazote or 2 to 3 sprigs or fresh thyme and/or marjoram (optional)

8 whole allspice or 2 teaspoons ground allspice, lightly toasted

1 teaspoon freshly ground black pepper

6 whole cloves or 1 teaspoon ground cloves

3 tablespoons vinegar (apple cider or rice)

2 teaspoons coarse salt

FOR THE SOUP

1 to 2 onions, roughly cut

2 stalks celery, diced

4 to 6 carrots, peeled and sliced

6 to 8 potatoes, peeled and cubed

1 cup red, white, or garbanzo beans, cooked (optional)

2 teaspoons salt

1 sprig of fresh epazote or 2 bay leaves

Fresh lime and queso fresco or cotija cheese

2. Place the meat in a nonreactive dish or pan and thoroughly spread the marinade on the meat. Cover and marinate for at least 2 hours or refrigerate overnight (much better).

3. Set up a pan or ovenproof bowl containing 2 1/2 quarts water or light broth, with a rack over the pan to catch the meat juices while cooking.

4. If you would like to make the soup, put some onions, celery, carrots, potatoes, and beans (optional) into the pan containing water or broth, along with 2 teaspoons salt and a sprig of fresh epazote or a couple of bay leaves.

5. For the meat, place two-thirds of the chard, cabbage, or banana leaves or the foil to cover the rack. Place the avocado leaves or the bay leaves and fennel or anise seed on the leaves, reserving some for the top of the meat. Place the meat on the rack, add the rest of the avocado leaves, or bay leaves and fennel or anise, and wrap with the remaining leaves or foil to create a loosely sealed package. If you are using foil, be sure to poke a few small holes with a fork in the bottom of the package to allow the juices to drain into the pan or bowl.

6. Put the pan or bowl with the rack and the package of wrapped meat in a preheated charcoal or gas grill with a lid, a 325-degree-F oven (a countertop electric roaster works great), or in a large steamer. Cook slowly until meat is fork-tender, almost soft. This will take 2 1/2 to 3 1/2 hours if the meat is cut in 3-inch chunks, 5 to 6 hours if it is whole, and 7 to 8 hours or more if it is a whole animal. Chicken will take about 1 3/4 to 2 1/2 hours.

7. Remove from heat and allow the meat to cool in the package for 30 to 45 minutes. Unwrap, remove the avocado or bay leaves and fennel, and hand-shred the meat, adding a little of the broth to keep it moist. Taste for salt and adjust if needed.

8. To serve the soup, skim the broth of excess fat, adjust the salt, and serve with fresh lime and queso fresco or cotija cheese.

Note: *Barbacoa is great as the meat for a make-your-own-tacos meal with fresh corn tortillas. It's good with an acidic salsa like Salsa Verde (see page 145), avocado slices, Mexican cheese, chopped white or red onions, limes, and, if you don't make the soup, some Frijoles de Olla (see page 128) or Frijoles Charros (see page 53).*

FOR THE MEAT

2 1/2 pounds Swiss chard leaves (or cabbage leaves, toasted banana leaves, rinsed and patted dry, or a piece of foil large enough to loosely wrap the meat)

20 dried avocado leaves (or 12 bay leaves along with 1 1/2 cups fresh fennel tops, coarsely chopped, or 2 tablespoons coarsely ground, toasted anise seed)

8 pounds lamb or young goat (bone-in shoulder or leg cuts are best)

La Tierra Maya

YUCATÁN, QUINTANA ROO, CAMPECHE, AND CHIAPAS

THE LAND OF THE MAYA comprises the states of Chiapas, Campeche, the Yucatán, Quintana Roo, and arguably parts of Tabasco. With the exception of Chiapas, with its varied terrain from high mountains to plains and low wetlands, most of this area is flat, forested, and tropical. On the Yucatán peninsula, there is an absence of surface rivers. Touching on both the Gulf of Mexico and the Caribbean Sea, this region is a contrast of the colonial and plantation cultures and the traditional Mayan culture.

Although typical Mexican dishes abound, the cooking is still very Mayan with influences from Europe, the Caribbean islands, Africa, and the Middle East. Though it has been over five hundred years since the first European visitors came, the Mayan culture is still surprisingly evident. Life in many towns and villages is more reminiscent of times past than of the twenty-first century, despite the technological gadgets and conveniences enjoyed by some. The Mayan language is alive and is spoken widely; Spanish is the second tongue of many natives.

Papadzules
YUCATÁN "ENCHILADAS" WITH TWO SAUCES

A STAPLE OF THE MAYAN YUCATÁN TABLE, these enchilada-like treats are simple and delicious with an exotic yet comforting flavor. Papadzules are made with two contrasting sauces: an herb-infused pumpkin-seed sauce and a tomato-chile sauce. The only additions since pre-Columbian times are the onions, garlic, and possibly the eggs. Usually served as an appetizer, they make a great main course with Frijoles Colados Yucateco (see page 189). You could also add cooked and shredded chicken or turkey in place of the eggs for a heartier version.

MAKES 8 SERVINGS

1. Boil the epazote in the salted water for 5 minutes. (Cilantro may be substituted for the epazote or added to intensify the flavor and green color. Do not boil the cilantro; rather add it after the seeds have been soaked in step 2.)

2. Mix the toasted and ground pumpkin seeds thoroughly with 1 cup of the hot epazote water and set aside for 10 to 15 minutes until greenish oil pools on the top. Carefully skim the oil and reserve it for garnish. (Not all varieties of pumpkin seeds yield enough oil to use for a garnish. Don't worry; the sauce will still taste good.)

3. Blend the pumpkin seeds with enough of the remaining epazote water to obtain a sauce with the consistency of thick gravy. Keep warm.

4. Blend the tomatoes with the habanero chile and garlic, and then strain. Fry the onion in the hot lard or oil until beginning to show some color, add the tomato-chile mixture, and salt and pepper to taste. Continue searing the sauce until it thickens slightly, 2 to 3

1 or 2 sprigs fresh or 2 tablespoons dried epazote

2 cups water, lightly salted

2 cups pumpkin seeds, 1 3/4 cups toasted and finely ground, and 1/4 cup toasted but left whole for garnish

6 to 8 ripe tomatoes, well charred (see page 27)

1 habanero chile, charred and stemmed (seeding is optional; leave in for traditional taste or take out to reduce heat)

4 to 6 cloves garlic, roasted and peeled (see page 23)

1 medium white onion, coarsely chopped

1 tablespoon lard or vegetable oil

Salt and pepper to taste

24 thin white corn tortillas

8 to 10 large eggs, hard-boiled, peeled, and chopped

minutes. Blend again and adjust the seasoning (you may add some of the epazote-infused water if the sauce is too thick). Keep warm.

5. Heat the tortillas on a comal or griddle until soft and pliable. Dip the hot tortillas into the pumpkin-seed sauce, place some of the hard-boiled eggs into each one, and roll up or fold in squares and set side-by-side on a serving platter. Pour over the remaining pumpkin-seed sauce and finally the tomato-chili sauce over the tortillas.

6. Garnish with the toasted pumpkin seeds, drops of the reserved pumpkin-seed oil, and Cebollas Moradas en Escabeche (see page 201).

Sopa de Lima
LIME SOUP WITH CHICKEN

CHICKEN SOUP IS KNOWN THE WORLD OVER as the cure-all for what ails you. It is the same in the Yucatán. This soup is just a little spicier. The hot and rich broth, flavorful chicken, and fiery chiles combine to make a comfort food that actually cools you down. Many people do not realize that although chiles initially taste hot, the effect on the body is to cause cooling. This is because the chiles cause a dilation of the capillaries and an increase in circulation. The hot sensation is merely the body releasing heat. That is why people who live in tropical climates tend to prefer spicy food. It also tastes good.

This soup has a variety of flavors that remain separate and distinct, since they are not cooked together for very long, yet complement each other well. You may prepare all of the separate parts beforehand and just heat up the broth to serve.

MAKES 8 MAIN-DISH SERVINGS

1. Heat the Caldo de Pollo with the lime slices and boil for 3 to 4 minutes.

2. Divide the remaining ingredients among 8 prewarmed soup bowls.

3. Ladle the broth (with or without the sliced lime) over the ingredients in each bowl.

4. Garnish with crispy strips of fried corn tortillas sprinkled on top of the soup or fresh corn tortillas on the side. Serve immediately.

2 1/2 quarts Caldo de Pollo (see page 138), salted

4 limes, thinly sliced

1 whole chicken, rubbed with Recado Colorado (see page 197) or achiote paste, roasted, skinned, stripped from the bone, and shredded

4 small to medium tomatoes, seeded and diced

1 medium red onion, rinsed and diced

1 to 2 habanero chiles, stemmed, seeded, and minced, or 2 to 3 serrano or jalapeño chiles, thinly sliced in rounds

2 to 3 ripe avocados, peeled and diced or sliced

1 bunch cilantro leaves, whole or coarsely chopped, or 32 whole fresh oregano leaves

Juice of 2 limes

Fried corn tortillas, cut into strips, or fresh corn tortillas on the side

Queso Relleno

BAKED GOUDA CHEESE STUFFED WITH SPICED MEAT

IN SPANISH-SPEAKING KITCHENS, the term *relleno* refers to something that is stuffed. Queso Relleno turns the typical chile relleno, which is stuffed with cheese, inside out. Queso Relleno is cheese that is stuffed with seasoned meat!

In days past, the Yucatán actually had more trade with Europe than with the rest of Mexico due to the lack of roads through the jungles of the area. The preference for Dutch cheeses is still evident today in Mérida, the capital. The Spanish and Creole influence is also shown in the picadillo and the gravy sauce. This recipe is my interpretation of the queso relleno that I tasted in Silvio Campo's little restaurant across from the mercado (store) in the Mayan town of Tixkokob, about an hour from Mérida.

MAKES 6 TO 8 SERVINGS

PICADILLO FILLING

1. Put meat in pan and cover with four cups of water. Bring to a boil with the onion, garlic, bay leaves, oregano, allspice, cloves, peppercorns, and salt. Lower the flame and cook for about 30 minutes if using ground meat (or 1 1/4 hours or until tender, if using chunks of meat). Strain the meat (shred if using chunks), remove the onion, garlic, spices, and herbs, and set the broth aside to cool.

2. Fry the onion, garlic, and sweet pepper in the lard or vegetable oil until soft but not brown.

3. Add the ground spices, tomatoes, raisins, almonds, olives, and capers, and fry another minute.

4. Add the vinegar and the meat and continue to cook until almost dry.

5. Add salt and pepper to taste and stir in the chopped eggs. Set aside.

FOR THE PICADILLO FILLING

2 1/2 pounds ground pork, pork butt, or pork shoulder

4 cups water

1 onion, quartered

2 cloves garlic

2 bay leaves, toasted

2 sprigs fresh mild oregano leaves or 1 tablespoon toasted Mexican oregano

4 whole allspice berries, toasted

3 cloves

6 whole black peppercorns

1 teaspoon salt

1 onion, finely chopped

3 cloves garlic, roasted, peeled, and chopped

1 sweet pepper or mild chile, seeded and chopped

4 tablespoons pork lard or vegetable oil

1/2 to 1 teaspoon ground canela

1/4 teaspoon ground cloves

4 to 6 whole allspice, toasted and ground

179

*5 to 6 tomatoes, lightly roasted,
peeled, seeded, and chopped*

1/4 cup raisins or currants

*1/4 cup almonds, lightly toasted,
peeled, and slivered*

*1/4 cup green olives, pitted
and chopped*

2 tablespoons capers

1/3 cup cider vinegar

*Salt and freshly ground black
pepper to taste*

3 hard-boiled eggs, chopped

FOR THE GRAVY

1/2 cup lard or butter

1/2 cup all-purpose flour

Pinch of ground cumin

Pinch of ground cloves

1 quart reserved pork broth

*1/2 onion, finely minced and
browned*

*1 tomato, peeled, seeded,
and finely chopped*

*Pinch of saffron or 1 teaspoon
toasted azafrán (optional)*

Salt and pepper to taste

GRAVY

1. Heat the lard or butter in a skillet or saucepan until it begins to sizzle. Whisk in the flour a little at a time until a smooth paste is formed. Add the cumin and cloves. Continue stirring while cooking for about 1 minute until a toasty aroma develops.

2. Remove from heat and whisk in the cool pork broth until smooth. Add the onion, tomato, and saffron. Return to heat and bring to a slow boil. Cook for about 5 minutes until thickened and smooth. Add salt and pepper to taste. Puree if desired.

TOMATO SAUCE

1. Fry the onion, green pepper or green or yellow chile, and garlic in the lard until soft but not brown.

2. Add the tomatoes, capers, and epazote and cook well.

3. Add the water and cook until the sauce thickens and the tomatoes soften. Remove the epazote. Blend smooth if desired. Add salt and pepper to taste.

RELLENO

1. Pare off the red waxy skin of the cheese with a sharp knife or peeler. Cut a 1/2-inch-thick slice off the top to make a lid. Hollow out the inside of the cheese (a melon ball tool is helpful for this) until the shell is about 1/2 inch thick.

2. Place the picadillo filling in the cheese and replace the lid. Wrap the cheese in the banana leaves or cheesecloth, tie it tightly with twine or thread, and heat in a bain-marie or double boiler in a preheated 350-degree-F oven for approximately 35 minutes.

3. To serve, unwrap the cheese, place it on a serving dish, and pour first the gravy then the sauce over and around it. Queso Relleno can be served as a main course, with tortillas for making tacos, or as an appetizer. Charred habanero salsa usually accompanies it.

Note: You can improvise the bain-marie by placing a covered roasting pan or casserole inside a larger pan containing 1 inch of water.

FOR THE TOMATO SAUCE

1/2 medium onion, chopped

1 green pepper or mild green or yellow chile, finely chopped

1 clove garlic, finely chopped

1 tablespoon pork lard

8 medium tomatoes, charred, peeled, seeded, and chopped

1 tablespoon capers

2 or 3 leaves fresh epazote (optional)

1/2 cup water

Salt and pepper to taste

FOR THE RELLENO

1 large or 6 to 8 small Edam or Gouda cheese balls

Banana leaves or cheesecloth to wrap the cheese

Tikin-Xic

MAYAN-STYLE GRILLED FISH

THIS FLAVORFUL AND COLORFUL FISH RECIPE is prepared along the coasts of the Yucatán and Quintana Roo. The usual method is to season a whole skin-on fillet of fish and wrap it in banana leaves with tomatoes, onions, sweet peppers, and chiles, and then char-grill the entire package. Individual serving packets can also be made, or you may just season individual portions and cook them directly over the coals without the wrapper.

MAKES 8 TO 10 SERVINGS

1. Combine the fruit juices and vinegar with the recado or achiote seasoning to make a soft paste.

2. Season the fish with salt and pepper and rub the paste all over the fish.

3. Toast the banana leaves to make them pliable and place them shiny side up on the counter.

4. Place the fish in the center of the banana leaves or foil; scatter the oregano or cilantro evenly over the fish; and cover with the tomatoes, peppers, onion, and chiles. Season with salt and pepper and drizzle with the olive or vegetable oil.

5. Wrap the banana leaves completely around the fish and tie with small strips of the leaf or use foil to make a sealed package.

6. Place over hot coals or in a 400-degree-F oven and cook for about 15 minutes, turn over the package, and cook 15 minutes more. Only cook about 7 to 10 minutes for individual portions.

7. Turn back to the original position and cook 10 to 15 minutes more until the fish is done.

8. Open the package carefully and spoon some of the juices that formed from cooking over the fish.

2/3 cup orange juice

2 tablespoons lime juice

1 tablespoon grapefruit juice

1 tablespoon vinegar (pineapple or apple cider)

6 ounces Recado Colorado (see page 197) or commercial achiote condiment

1 whole fish fillet, 3 to 5 pounds, skin on or 8 to 10 individually portioned fillets

Salt and pepper

Several large banana leaves or heavy-duty aluminum foil

1 1/2 tablespoons fresh oregano or cilantro leaves

3 to 4 roma tomatoes, sliced

1 to 2 sweet red or yellow bell peppers, cleaned and cut in 1-inch strips

1 large red onion, peeled and cut in thin slices, or 1/2 cup Cebollas Moradas en Escabeche (see page 201)

2 or 3 yellow, hot, jalapeño, or fresno chiles split lengthwise, or 1 to 2 whole habanero chiles

3 to 4 tablespoons olive or vegetable oil

Carne Asada Yucateca

GRILLED PORK STEAK WITH ACHIOTE AND CHILES

I HAD THIS DISH AT SILVIO CAMPO'S restaurant in Tixkokob, Yucatán, with my Mayan friend Maximiliano Chuc. Traditional Mexican carne asada is usually made with beef and is not as highly seasoned, but this version with pork is outstanding. You can cook it on a griddle or skillet, but I prefer to cook it on an outdoor or indoor grill. Serve it with tortillas, pickled red onions, guacamole, charred chiles, and green onions, lime wedges, and Frijoles Colados Yucatecos (see page 189).

MAKES 8 SERVINGS

1. Combine all of the ingredients except the pork to make a paste.

2. Rub the paste all over the pork and let sit 2 hours to overnight.

3. Cook on a hot griddle, comal, or grill until just cooked through.

3 to 4 pounds pork steaks, thinly sliced, or boneless pork chops, pounded thin

1 tablespoon Recado Colorado (see page 197) or achiote paste with 1 teaspoon ground allspice

2 habanero or other hot chiles, charred, seeded, and finely chopped

6 cloves garlic, minced

2 teaspoons Mexican oregano, toasted

1 teaspoon salt

1/2 teaspoon ground black pepper

1 teaspoon sugar

Juice of 1/2 orange

1 teaspoon vinegar (pineapple or apple cider)

1 tablespoon vegetable oil

Brazo de la Reina
QUEEN'S ARM TAMALE

THIS IS THE UNUSUAL TAMALE that I first tasted at Eladio's, a popular local Yucatecán restaurant in Mérida, where white-clad waiters serve authentic snacks and main dishes under a thatched palapa canopy while the diners enjoy live music. The tamale is cooked in one large roll to resemble an arm and is then usually cut in finger-size pieces and served on a banana leaf.

MAKES 8 SERVINGS AS A MAIN COURSE

1. Toast the banana leaves to make them pliable. Lay them out, shiny-side-up and overlapping, to form a 24 x 12-inch rectangle.

2. Spread the masa evenly in the center of the leaves in an 8 x 16–inch rectangle.

3. Sprinkle 2/3 of the pumpkin seeds in a 2-inch-wide strip down the center of the masa.

4. Lay the egg slices on top of the pumpkin seeds in one row.

5. Roll up the tamale by first folding the leaf away from you until the two edges of the masa meet. Fold in the two ends to the edge of the masa. Tuck the roll in firmly and finish rolling up in a log shape. If necessary, add more banana leaves to ensure the tamale is well sealed. You may use strips of the leaves to secure the tamale.

6. Create a double boiler or bain-marie out of two roasting or other pans that will nest together and accommodate the tamale. Place 1 1/2 inches of water in the first pan, and then nest the second pan on top. Place the tamale in the second pan and cover with foil or a tight-fitting lid. Bake in the oven at 350 degrees F for 50 to 60 minutes. (You may also cook on the stovetop, but be sure to keep water in the pan at all times.)

3 or 4 large banana leaves plus extra for serving

Recipe for the masa portion of Tamalitos Chayas (see page 192) prepared through step 2, adding the cooked greens to the masa instead of reserving

1 1/4 cups pumpkin seeds, toasted and ground

8 eggs, hard-boiled, peeled, and cut in 1/2-inch slices

Batch of tomato sauce from Queso Relleno (see page 179), omitting the capers and using the epazote

7. Cool the tamale for 10 minutes or so and then carefully unwrap.

8. Cut into slices or finger shapes for serving.

9. To serve, place several slices of tamale on a banana leaf, top each serving with the warm tomato sauce, and sprinkle with the remaining pumpkin seeds.

Frijoles Colados Yucateco
YUCATÁN-STYLE SIEVED BLACK BEANS

IN THE YUCATÁN, black beans are passed through a sieve to remove the skins and make them smooth. These are very different from the simply smashed refried beans from other regions of the country. The black beans are then cooked slowly until thick and used as a side dish, a sauce, or a filling for antojitos (snacks).

MAKES 8 TO 10 SERVINGS

1. After making the Frijoles de Olla, remove the habanero chile and reserve if still intact. Discard the epazote and avocado leaves or hoja santa.

2. Puree the beans in a blender until smooth.

3. Pass the beans through a fine sieve or strainer (if you do not have a strainer that works well for this, you may omit this step).

4. In a preheated heavy pot, sauté the onion in the oil or lard with the pinch of salt until color just begins to develop. Add the strained beans and the reserved habanero chile (or a fresh whole habanero chile).

5. Cook over medium-low heat, stirring often until the beans form a thick paste.

1 batch Frijoles de Olla (see page 128), cooked with double the epazote; the habanero chile; and the avocado leaves, hoja santa, or ground anise

1 small to medium onion, very thinly sliced in strips

1 to 2 tablespoons vegetable oil or lard

Pinch of salt

Ensalada de Chiles Xicatiques Rellenos
SALAD WITH PORK-STUFFED YELLOW CHILES

The Yaxche restaurant in Playa del Carmen, Quintana Roo, was where I first tried this recipe. The flavors, colors, and textures create a dish that is so sophisticated that I was convinced it was a contemporary take on Mayan food. However, after researching more, I found out that it is quite traditional. The young chef at Yaxche corrected me when I described it as Yucatecan cuisine. "This is Mayan cooking," he said. A subtle distinction to be sure, but very important to the locals. You may use many varieties of fresh chiles, meat fillings, and greens. The chef used Chaya, a native Mayan green, but I have made it often with the alternatives. I add toasted pumpkin seeds or tortilla strips for crunchiness.

MAKES 6 SERVINGS

1. Stuff the chiles with the meat and heat for about 6 to 8 minutes in a 350-degree-F oven or until heated through.

2. Blend the orange and lime juices, vinegar, achiote, cilantro, oil, and salt and pepper in a blender or with a whisk.

3. Place the greens on plates, top with the chiles, drizzle with the dressing, and serve.

12 xicatic, yellow hot, Anaheim, New Mexican green, or other fresh chiles, roasted, peeled and seeded

1 1/2 pounds Cochinita Pibil (see page 202), shredded*

Juice of 1 orange

2 tablespoons lime juice

1 tablespoon vinegar (pineapple or apple cider)

1/2 teaspoon achiote paste or Recado Colorado (see page 197)

2 tablespoons cilantro, chopped

1/4 cup olive oil

Salt and pepper

2 pounds chaya, spinach, or mixed baby greens, washed

*You may substitute shredded chicken or a different recipe for the pork.

Tamalitos Chayas
LITTLE TAMALES WITH GREENS

FOR THE TAMALES

2 pounds chaya leaves or spinach, Swiss chard, beet greens, or collard greens, stems removed and cut into pieces 2 inches across

2 quarts water, lightly salted

2 1/2 pounds fresh masa or prepared masa for tamales (see page 29)

1 pound lard (or if making the vegetarian version 1/2 pound shortening and 1/2 pound butter)

1 teaspoon salt

32 rectangles of banana leaves (10 inches long x 8 inches wide)* plus extra for ties

*32 cornhusks, soaked, may be substituted

FOR THE GARNISH

Pumpkin seeds, ground and toasted

Chopped egg

Crumbled cheese

I FIRST TASTED THESE LITTLE TAMALES in a vegetarian coffee house called La Jara in Palenque, Chiapas, the small town outside of the spectacular Mayan ruins of the same name. This was one of the more important cradles of Mesoamerican ancient civilization. In the area, you can witness the mixing of the indigenous styles of mountainous Chiapas with the lowland and Gulf Coast cooking of Tabasco and the Yucatán. This tamale version contains pork, but you can easily make a vegetarian version using the instructions in the recipe. Tamalitos Chayas are similar to a vegetarian Yucatán tamale, which are also made with chaya leaves, but are filled with pumpkin seeds and hard-boiled eggs. Although the flavor of spinach is similar to chaya, more durable greens often make a better substitute.

MAKES 32 TAMALES

1. Cook the chaya or other greens in the 2 quarts of boiling salted water until they are tender, taking care that they do not become too soft. Drain and reserve the water.

2. Strain the reserved water in which the Chaya leaves were cooked through a cheesecloth or fine sieve. Mix with the masa. Gently heat the mixture in a heavy saucepan or Dutch oven until it comes to a boil, then add the lard and salt to taste. Cook the mixture, stirring often (a wooden spoon works well for this), for 15 to 20 minutes or until cooked through and smooth. You can tell it is ready when a small amount is pressed on a banana leaf and it pulls away easily and cleanly.

3. Place the pork in a pan with 2 cups of water along with the herbs and the onion until it is cooked (approximately 20 minutes). Drain and remove the herbs and onion.

4. Heat the lard or oil and fry the pureed tomato and onion. After 1 minute, add the remaining ingredients, including the meat. Simmer over a low flame until the mixture has thickened. Salt and pepper to taste.

5. Toast the banana leaves over an open flame or on a comal or griddle until the inside of the leaf turns shiny and becomes pliable (see page 29).

6. Place some chaya or other leaves on top of the banana-leaf rectangles, add a large tablespoon of cooked masa, and spread about 3 x 3 inches. Place another 2 tablespoons of the filling on top, cover with another chaya leaf, and form the tamales by folding the side ends of the leaf in towards the center. Do the same with the ends until a small rectangular package is formed. Use strips of the leaves to secure the bundle, if you like.

7. Place each tamale lengthwise in a tamale steamer or plain steamer. Repeat this process until you have used up the entire filling, making sure to leave a little space around each of the tamales to allow the air to circulate. Steam for 1 1/4 hours or until the tamales come off the banana leaf easily when they are unwrapped.

8. Serve the tamales arranged on a platter, with sauce over the top and sprinkle with ground, toasted pumpkin seeds, and chopped egg or crumbled cheese.

FOR THE FILLING

2 1/2 pounds ground pork

2 cups water

3 bay leaves

2 sprigs epazote (or 2 sprigs oregano and 2 sprigs fresh thyme or 2 tablespoons toasted Mexican oregano)

1 teaspoon whole allspice, toasted and ground

1 medium white onion

1 tablespoon lard or vegetable oil

2 1/2 pounds ripe tomatoes, pureed with 1/2 white onion and strained

1 1/2 cups pimento-stuffed green olives, chopped

2 tablespoons capers

2/3 cup raisins

2 sweet red peppers or 1 green pepper, seeded and diced

1 hot yellow, jalapeño, or serrano chile, seeded and finely minced

Salt and pepper to taste

FOR THE SAUCE

1 medium white onion,
   thinly sliced

2 tablespoons lard or
   vegetable oil

3 pounds tomatoes, roasted

3 xicatic chiles (or 2 güero or hot
   yellow chiles, or 1 chile
   habanero, roasted, peeled, and
   seeded)

1 sprig epazote (optional)

Salt and pepper to taste

1. Sauté the onion in the lard or the oil until translucent.

2. Puree the onions, tomato, and chile, then fry the mixture until it is thickened.

3. Add salt and pepper to taste.

Tres Recados Yucatecos
THE THREE BASIC YUCATÁN SEASONING PASTES

Most cooks in the Yucatán use the Tres Recados described here as the base flavor of much of their cooking—whether they prepare them at home or purchase them in the local markets. Each is simply a paste formed by grinding together a mixture of spices and flavorings to be used as a seasoning. Although there are more than three seasoning pastes, as well as many variations, these three are the most important and can be supplemented with other spices to accommodate many cooking needs.

The three flavors used in these pastes are (1) *colorado* (red) for seafood and all-around use; (2) *negro* (black) for Chilmole, Pavo en Relleno Negro, and various other plates; and (3) *de bistec* (for beefsteak), used to season many meats (not only beef) and often seafood. In the markets in Mérida, Valladolid, and Chetumal, and in smaller village markets around the peninsula, you can see colorful mounds of the various seasoning pastes displayed for sale.

Recado Colorado
RED SEASONING PASTE

THIS RED SEASONING PASTE is available commercially in the United States and Mexico. The store-bought versions, usually labeled *Condimento de Achiote*, are quite serviceable (I use them a lot), but it is nice to create the homemade variety with its distinct flavors.

The annatto seeds are pretty tough. If you do not have a molcajete or a very powerful spice grinder, I recommend using the prepared achiote. Remember, the paste may not be used immediately so do not toast the spices.

MAKES ABOUT 1 CUP

1. Mix the annatto seeds with the 2 tablespoons of vinegar and soak for several hours.

2. Finely grind the annatto seeds and the rest of the ingredients separately in a molcajete or durable spice grinder.

3. Mix until a smooth, stiff paste is formed, adding more vinegar as needed.

4. Form into a block or circular disks, wrap well, and refrigerate to store.

1/3 cup annatto seeds (achiote)

2 tablespoons apple cider vinegar, plus more as needed

8 whole allspice berries

1 teaspoon coriander seeds (optional)

2 teaspoons whole black pepper

1/4 teaspoon cumin seed

1/2 teaspoon whole cloves

12 to 14 cloves garlic, peeled

1 tablespoon Mexican oregano

1 1/2 teaspoons salt

Recado Negro
BLACK SEASONING PASTE

1/8 cup annatto seeds (achiote)

2 tablespoons apple cider vinegar, plus more as needed

12 to 16 ancho (mild), mulato (medium), or guajillo (hot) chiles (or a mix of all three), toasted very dark, stemmed, and seeded

6 whole allspice berries

1/2 stick canela (optional)

2 teaspoons whole black pepper

1/2 teaspoon whole cloves

20 cloves garlic, peeled

1 tablespoon Mexican oregano

1 1/2 teaspoons salt

MAKES ABOUT 2 CUPS

1. Mix the annatto seeds with the 2 tablespoons of vinegar and soak for several hours.

2. Finely grind all of the ingredients separately in a molcajete or durable spice grinder.

3. Mix until a smooth paste is formed, adding more vinegar as needed.

4. Form into a block or circular disks, wrap well, and refrigerate to store.

Recado de Bistec
BEEFSTEAK SEASONING PASTE

1. Finely grind all of the ingredients, except the vinegar, in a molcajete or durable spice grinder.

2. Mix until a smooth, stiff paste is formed, adding vinegar as needed.

3. Form into a block or circular disks, wrap well, and refrigerate to store.

2 teaspoons coriander seeds

1 tablespoon whole allspice berries

1 stick canela

2 tablespoons whole black pepper

1 teaspoon whole cloves

12 cloves garlic, peeled

1 tablespoon Mexican oregano

2 teaspoons salt

Apple cider vinegar, as needed

Cebollas Moradas en Escabeche
PICKLED RED ONIONS

THESE ONIONS ARE A FUNDAMENTAL COMPONENT of the majority of dishes in the Yucatán cooking repertoire, and their striking color and crunchy texture make them a suitable garnish for many other Mexican plates as well. They will keep for several months in the refrigerator and are easy to can for long-term storage.

MAKES ABOUT 3 CUPS

1. Place everything except the onions in a nonreactive saucepan. Bring to a boil and cook for 7 minutes. Remove the orange and reserve.

2. Put the onions in a bowl. Pour the hot mixture over the onions and stir well.

   Note: You may strain the liquid to remove the spices before adding to the onions if you prefer. (I like the rustic quality and added flavor gained by leaving them in.)

3. Juice the orange and add the juice to the bowl of onions. Stir again to ensure that the onions are completely submerged. Stirring several more times, cool to room temperature. Refrigerate. (If canning, add the orange juice, skip the cooling, pour into the canning jars, and follow canning instructions for heating and sealing.)

   Note: Before serving, allow the onions to warm to room temperature. They'll taste better.

1 cup vinegar (apple cider, rice, or pineapple)

1/2 cup water

1 clove garlic

1 teaspoon whole allspice, toasted

2 teaspoons black peppercorns, toasted

4 whole cloves

1 2-inch piece canela

4 bay leaves, toasted

1 or 2 sprigs of fresh thyme and/or marjoram

1 habanero chile, lightly charred (optional)

2 tablespoons piloncillo or raw sugar

1 tablespoon salt

1 orange or tangerine, unpeeled

3 large red onions, peeled and sliced 1/4 inch thick in rounds or strips

Cochinita Pibil
PIT-ROASTED PORK

1 medium (4 to 6 pound) boneless
   pork butt or arm roast, trimmed
   but with some fat remaining

3 ounces achiote paste or Recado
   Colorado (see page 197) (use
   only half the allspice and
   oregano)

12 cloves garlic, peeled

1 medium white onion, coarsely
   chopped (3/4 cup)

2 tablespoons allspice berries,
   toasted and cracked, or 1
   tablespoon ground allspice

2 tablespoons Mexican oregano,
   toasted

1 teaspoon cumin seed, toasted
   and crushed

2 teaspoons cracked black pepper

6 bay leaves, toasted

2 tablespoons Worcestershire
   sauce (optional)

Juice of 2 limes

Juice of 1 orange

1/4 cup vinegar (pineapple, apple
   cider, or rice)

PIBIL IS THE MAYAN word for a pit that is dug in the ground and lined with stones to roast a suckling pig. A fire is built and allowed to burn for several hours until it is reduced to smoldering coals. Meanwhile, the *cochinita*, or little pig, has been seasoned and marinated with the exotic flavors of the brick-red achiote, the bright taste of citrus, and the floral heat of the habanero chile. Wrapped in banana leaves, the meat is placed in the pit, covered with the rocks and some palm leaves or wet burlap, and slow-roasted overnight. This feast is served family-style with fresh handmade tortillas, salsas, condiments, and salads.

Cochinita Pibil is a festive meal, excellent for parties and gatherings. The long, unattended cooking period allows time in the kitchen for the preparation of salsas, condiments, and side dishes. I developed this recipe to provide the home cook with a close and good alternative to pit cooking. I have also had success using the combination of a backyard smoker for the first 1 1/2 hours and the indoor oven for about 3 more hours to finish the cooking. Although the banana leaves lend a distinct flavor to the meat as well as a dramatic presentation, aluminum foil also produces an outstanding dish.

MAKES 3 1/2 TO 4 POUNDS COOKED PORK

1. Make several 1-inch-deep cuts on the fat side of the pork to allow the marinade to penetrate. Place the meat in a freezer bag, other large plastic bag, or a large nonreactive container.

2. Mix all the other ingredients except the banana leaves in a blender or food processor. Pour in with the pork, seal bag, and distribute well to coat the meat. Marinate at least 2 hours or overnight in the refrigerator.

3. Preheat oven to 325 degrees F.

4. Thaw and rinse the frozen banana leaves well in cool water. Tear eight 1/2-inch-wide strips off one leaf and tie two together to make four strips to use later for ties. Toast the banana leaves to make them more pliable (see page 29). Line the bottom of a heavy roasting pan with 2 or 3 of the banana leaves. They should overlap the pan on all sides.

5. Remove the pork roast from the bag and reserve the marinade.

6. Place pork fat-side-up on banana leaves in the pan. Pour about 1/2 cup of the marinade over top of the meat.

7. Place 3 or 4 more leaves over the pork and inside the bottom leaves. Pull bottom leaves around the meat and tie strips of banana leaves around this package from both directions to secure.

Note: If you are smoking the meat first, you may want to place the package that is wrapped in banana leaves on a sheet of aluminum foil to catch any leaks.

8. Bake at 325 degrees F for 3 1/2 to 4 hours until meat is fork-tender. Leaves will be darkened on the outside when finished.

9. Allow to cool for 20 minutes. Slit open the banana leaves with a sharp knife or scissors (be careful of the steam) and remove the pork or present on the leaves.

10. Serve with fresh corn tortillas or Salsa Fresca (see page 143), Cebollas Moradas en Escabeche (see page 201), sliced radishes, chopped cilantro, citrus wedges, guacamole, and jicama salad.

2 to 3 fresh habanero or Scotch bonnet chiles, stems and seeds removed (or 2 to 3 tablespoons bottled habanero chile sauce)

2 tablespoons vegetable oil

2 tablespoons salt

1 package (1 pound) frozen banana leaves or heavy-duty aluminum foil

Panuchos Quintana Roo

BEAN-FILLED CORN TORTILLAS TOPPED WITH CHICKEN OR TURKEY AND GARNISHES

FOR THE MEAT

2 ounces Recado Colorado (see page 197)

1/2 cup Seville orange juice, or a mixture of regular orange juice and 1 tablespoon cider vinegar

1/2 habanero or serrano chile, seeded and finely minced (optional)

1 medium-size chicken, jointed and skinned, or 2 turkey legs and thigh sections

Salt and pepper

MANY DIFFERENT VERSIONS OF PANUCHOS, another of the countless corn masa snacks, can be found throughout Mexico, especially in the central and southern states. Panuchos are a freshly cooked corn tortilla filled with refried beans and sometimes sliced hard-cooked eggs, then fried or baked, and topped with shredded meat and condiments. Although the traditional fresh tortillas undoubt-edly produce the best results, store-bought white corn tortillas may be used. Since the store-bought variety usually don't puff up like the homemade ones, simply fold them over the filling, or sandwich the filling between two whole tortillas, and proceed according to the recipe. The version here is from Mexico's newest state on the Caribbean side of the Yucatán peninsula, Quintana Roo. Panuchos lend themselves well to the creative use of left-overs since any number of meats and garnishes may be employed.

MAKES 8 SERVINGS

1. Preheat the oven to 365 degrees F.

2. Dissolve the recado in the orange juice in a bowl or pan and mix in the chile if using.

3. Add the chicken or turkey, coat evenly, and season with salt and pepper.

4. Place the seasoned meat in a roasting pan or casserole dish and cover tightly.

5. Bake for 30 minutes. Remove the cover and continue to bake for about 20 to 25 minutes more until the chicken is cooked through and most of the moisture has evaporated.

6. Cool and finely shred. Set aside.

204

TO ASSEMBLE

1. Make small tortillas (see instructions on page 121) on a comal or griddle.

2. Make a pocket in each tortilla by lifting up the layer of masa that has puffed up, fill with the refried bean, and press the layer down again.

3. Fry in hot lard or oil until golden brown on both sides, drain on paper towels, add salt to taste.

4. Top each bean-filled corn tortilla with chicken or turkey meat and other garnishes as desired.

FOR THE TORTILLAS

2 cups dry masa harina

1/2 teaspoon salt

1 7/8 cup (approximately) warm water (95 to 115 degree F)

3 cups refried black beans or Frijoles Colados Yucatecos (see page 189)

Pork lard or corn oil for frying

Salt to taste

FOR THE GARNISH

3 medium-size tomatoes, peeled and diced

2 avocados, peeled and diced

1 small white cabbage or head of iceberg lettuce, finely sliced

1 jalapeño or hot yellow chile, stemmed, seeded, and thinly sliced

4 to 6 sliced radishes

Cebollas Moradas en Escabeche (see page 201)

Chopped cilantro

Lime wedges or slices

Chile Poblano Rajas
PICKLED FIRE-ROASTED POBLANO CHILES

3 medium or 2 large poblano
    chiles, roasted, peeled, stemmed,
    seeded, and cooled (see page 21)

2 tablespoons lime juice or mild
    vinegar (pineapple, rice, or
    apple cider)

1/2 teaspoon salt or to taste

A few drops vegetable oil
    (optional)

CHILE RAJAS are little strips of roasted and peeled chiles (usually poblano), that are pickled and used in tacos, as a condiment for grilled meats, and as a complement to many other Mexican dishes. New Mexican, Anaheim, jalapeño, and other chiles may also be used.

MAKES ABOUT 1 CUP

1. Cut the chiles into 1/4-inch-wide long strips.

2. Toss with the lime juice or vinegar.

3. Season with salt.

4. Let marinate for 30 minutes, and then add the oil to help preserve the chiles and make them shiny.

Chile Poblano Rajas
WARM FIRE-ROASTED POBLANO CHILES

I HAVE INCLUDED A CONTEMPORARY VARIATION of this recipe using sweet green, red, yellow, or purple peppers along with the chiles, and some mushrooms and onions. Warm Chile Poblano Rajas may be used in tacos or as a condiment to meat; they may also be used as a vegetable side dish. New Mexico green chiles or Anaheim chiles may be substituted for the Poblanos.

MAKES ABOUT 3 CUPS

1. Cut the chiles and peppers into 1/4-inch-wide long strips

2. Place the oil in a preheated pan; add the mushrooms when the oil begins to smoke. Sauté on high heat until well-browned, and then remove from pan.

3. Sauté the onions on medium-low heat until golden-brown around the edges. (You may need a little more oil for this.)

4. Add the chile rajas, marjoram or oregano, and mushrooms, heat through, and add the caldo.

5. Bring to a boil and continue cooking until most of the liquid is evaporated.

6. Season with salt and serve.

3 medium or 2 large poblano chiles, roasted, peeled, stemmed, and seeded (see page 21)

2 sweet bell peppers (any color), roasted, peeled, stemmed, and seeded

2 to 3 tablespoons olive or vegetable oil

3/4 cup sliced mushrooms

1 white onion, peeled and cut into long strips

2 teaspoons fresh sweet marjoram leaves or toasted Mexican oregano

1/2 cup Caldo de Res or Caldo de Pollo (see pages 140, 138)

Salt to taste

INGREDIENT AND EQUIPMENT SOURCES

Santa Fe School of Cooking
116 West San Francisco Street
Santa Fe, NM 87501
telephone: (505) 983-4511
www.santafeschoolofcooking.com
cookin@santafeschoolofcooking.com

Ingredients, equipment, and utensils.
You can also register for cooking classes with the author or other instructors.

Burns Farms
1345 Bay Lake Loop
Groveland, FL 34736
telephone: (352) 429-4048

A great source for fresh hoja santa (acuyo) when in season.

The CMC Company
P.O. Drawer 322
Avalon, NJ 08202
telephone: (800) CMC-2780
fax: (609)-861-3065
www.thecmccompany.com

Large selection of Mexican ingredients and equipment.

Gourmet Sleuth
telephone: (408) 354-8281
www.gourmetsleuth.com

Mexican and other ingredients and equipment.

Mex Grocer
www.mexgrocer.com

Ingredients and equipment.

Melissa's
telephone: (800) 468-7111

Fresh and dried chiles, cornhusks, tomatillos, and other necessities.

Don Alfonso Foods
telephone: (800) 456-6100

Chiles, prepared moles, and other items.

Frieda's by Mail
4465 Corporate Center Drive
Los Alamitos, CA 90720
telephone: (800) 421-9477
www.friedas.com

Fresh and dried chiles.

Herbs of Mexico
3903 Whittier Boulevard
Los Angeles, CA 90023
telephone: (213) 261-2521

Dried herbs and spices, such as epazote.

Kitchen Market
218 Eighth Avenue
New York, NY 10011
telephone: (212) 243-4433
fax: (888) HOT-4433
www.kitchenmarket.com

Canela, Mexican oregano, and avocado leaves.

Generation Farms
1109 North McKinney
Rice, Texas 75155
telephone: (903) 326-4263
fax: (903) 326-6511

Fresh epazote and hoja santa (1/2-pound minimum, but 1/4-pound if you order several herbs).

Penzey's Ltd.
telephone: (800) 741-7787
fax: (262) 679-7878
www.penzeys.com

Canela, dried epazote and Mexican oregano, and chipotle chiles.

Valley Food Warehouse
14530 Nordhoff
Panorama City, CA 91402
telephone: (818) 891-9939
fax: (818) 891-1781

Avocado leaves, epazote, and banana leaves, as well as other Mexican and Central American ingredients.

Plaza Piaxtla
898 Flushing Avenue
Brooklyn, NY 11206
telephone: (718) 386-2626

Good source for equipment and Mexican ingredients including fresh epazote and dried hoja santa.

Stop 1 Supermarket
210 W. 94th Street
New York 10025
telephone: (212) 864-9456

Large selection of Mexican chiles and seasonings, including dried avocado leaves, hoja santa, epazote, and canela.

Index

Culinary Adventure Tours

DANIEL HOYER LEADS FOOD AND CULTURAL ADVENTURES IN MEXICO, where you will get a chance to cook with locals and restaurant chefs. The trips also include market tours, cultural insights, nature appreciation, and visits to archeological sites as well as lots of great food. Join Daniel for an insider's view of this diverse and exciting country. Information and schedules are available at www.welleatenpath.com.